Magical Book

Magical Book

Divine ways to live your life wisely

Nicole Sommesous

Thorsons

Thorsons
An Imprint of HarperCollinsPublishers
77-85 Fulham Palace Road,
Hammersmith, London W6 8JB

The Thorsons website address is:
www.thorsons.com

First published 1999

10 9 8 7 6 5 4 3

©1999 Nicole Sommesous

Nicole Sommesous asserts her moral right to be identified as the author of this work.

A catalogue record for this book is available from the British Library

ISBN 0 7225 3898 7

Printed and bound in Great Britain by
Martins the Printers Limited, Berwick upon Tweed

The information in this book forms part of a collection gathered by the author over many years. For this reason not all the sources are traceable. The publishers are anxious to hear from any copyright holders who have not been contacted for permission.

All rights reserved. No part of this publication may be reproduced, stored in a retrieval system, or transmitted, in any form or by any means, electronic, mechanical, photocopying, recording or otherwise, without the prior permission of the publishers.

I thank my daughter, Florence, for sharing her time to help develop and translate this book with me.

I thank her for her understanding, for motivating me and for her positive spirit.

Contents

Astrology

Astrological Birthsigns	1
Ruling Elements	2
Your Ascendant Sign	3
Ascendant Star Chart	4
Star Signs	8
Birthsigns of Friends and Relatives	10
Your Day of Birth	12
Star Signs and the Planets	15
Planets in your Body	18
Your Health in your Star Sign	19
Star Signs and Physical Fragility	20
Astrology in your Kitchen	21
Star Affinities	24
Astrological Summary	26
Chinese Astrology	28
Egyptian Astrology	34

Divination

Divination by Runes	43
Cowrie Shells	48
Reading Matches	52
Numerology	53
Palm Reading	57

Using a Pendulum	58
Ouija	59
Tarot	60
Dominoes	66

Invoking Help

Guardian Angels	69
Angels to Pray to for Help	72
Good Genies	73
Charms for Luck and Protection	75

Natural Magic

Chakras	77
Yin or Yang?	81
Essential Oils	83
Planets and Scents	85
Magic Plants and Herbs	86
Honey	91
Incense	92
Candles	93
The Power of the Moon	97
The Power of the Sun	99

Practical Magic

| Strategies to Attract Money | 101 |
| Lotteries and Games of Chance | 102 |

Planets, Star Signs and Careers	103
Strange But True!	106
Pentacles	109
Aphrodisiacs	110
Babies	114
Granting of Wishes	116
Health	119
Protection	124
Inauspicious Dates	130
Wedding Anniversaries	131
Pyramids	132

Introduction

My name is Nicole Sommesous. I was born in France in the 1930s and started travelling as an infant. My father was a pilot in the French airforce and we spent some time in northern Africa.

In my twenties, I continued travelling extensively throughout Europe - to Greece, Italy, Finland, Yugoslavia and Great Britain. Married, with two children, I returned to Africa and spent the next 18 years travelling through Mauritania, Morocco, Mali, Chad, Cameroon, Senegal and Burkina Faso. I sometimes lived in the remotest villages and here I learned some of the local customs, beliefs and magic spells.

Divorced, and with my two children happily married with children of their own, I decided to head for the West Indies in the early 1990s, settling in Guadeloupe. I enjoyed island-hopping for a further seven years, continuing to accumulate knowledge of local magic arts and customs.

I have been a psychic tarot reader for more than 20 years now and am constantly asked by my clients for help, protection and guidance for very particular cases. So I decided to compile a pocketsize book of reference for myself, which I carry everywhere with me. I thought how useful it would be for people to have their own copy for their own use and reference.

I hope you will treasure this little almanac of magic the way I do mine!

Nicole

ASTROLOGICAL BIRTHSIGNS

SIGNS	DATE
Aries	March 22 - April 19
Taurus	April 20 - May 20
Gemini	May 21 - June 21
Cancer	June 22 - July 22
Leo	July 23 – August 22
Virgo	August 23 – September 21
Libra	September 22 – October 21
Scorpio	October 22 – November 21
Sagittarius	November 22 – December 21
Capricorn	December 22 – January 20
Aquarius	January 21 – February 19
Pisces	February 20 – March 21

RULING ELEMENTS

Fire: *Aries, Leo and Sagittarius*

Fire signs are characterized by movement, obsession and energy

Air: *Gemini, Libra and Aquarius*

Air signs are characterized by receptivity, intellect and aspirations

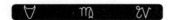

Earth: *Taurus, Virgo and Capricorn*

Earth signs are characterized by function, practicality and solidity

Water: *Cancer, Scorpio and Pisces*

Water signs are characterized by perception, intuition and day dreaming

YOUR ASCENDANT SIGN

Your ascendant sign is the sign that was rising over the eastern horizon at the moment you were born; it shows the 'external' you - the you that you show to the world!

Your ascendant sign depends upon your date of birth, and the hour of your birth.

Aries   *Taurus*   *Gemini*   *Cancer*   *Leo*   *Virgo*

Libra   *Scorpio*   *Sagittarius*   *Capricorn*   *Aquarius*   *Pisces*

ASCENDANT STAR CHART

Signs	Aries			Taurus			Gemini			Cancer			Leo			Virgo		
Decan	21.03 to 30.03	31.03 to 09.04	10.04 to 20.04	21.04 to 30.04	01.05 to 10.05	11.05 to 20.05	21.05 to 30.05	31.05 to 09.06	10.06 to 21.06	22.06 to 01.07	02.07 to 11.07	12.07 to 22.07	23.07 to 01.08	02.08 to 11.08	12.08 to 23.08	24.08 to 01.09	02.09 to 12.09	13.09 to 22.09
Hours																		
0.00	♐	♐	♐	♐	♑	♑	♒	♒	♓	♈	♈	♉	♉	♊	♊	♋	♋	♋
1 a.m.	♐	♐	♑	♑	♑	♒	♒	♓	♈	♉	♉	♊	♊	♊	♋	♋	♋	♌
2 a.m.	♐	♑	♑	♒	♒	♓	♓	♈	♉	♉	♊	♊	♋	♋	♋	♋	♌	♌
3 a.m.	♑	♑	♒	♒	♓	♈	♈	♉	♊	♊	♊	♋	♋	♋	♌	♌	♌	♌
4 a.m.	♑	♒	♓	♓	♈	♉	♉	♊	♊	♋	♋	♋	♋	♌	♌	♌	♌	♍
5 a.m.	♒	♓	♈	♈	♉	♊	♊	♊	♋	♋	♋	♋	♌	♌	♌	♌	♍	♍
6 a.m.	♓	♈	♉	♉	♊	♊	♋	♋	♋	♋	♌	♌	♌	♌	♍	♍	♍	♍
7 a.m.	♈	♉	♉	♊	♊	♋	♋	♋	♋	♌	♌	♌	♌	♍	♍	♍	♍	♎
8 a.m.	♉	♊	♊	♋	♋	♋	♋	♌	♌	♌	♌	♍	♍	♍	♍	♎	♎	♎
9 a.m.	♊	♊	♋	♋	♋	♋	♌	♌	♌	♌	♍	♍	♍	♍	♎	♎	♎	♎
10 a.m.	♊	♋	♋	♋	♌	♌	♌	♌	♍	♍	♍	♍	♎	♎	♎	♎	♏	♏
11 a.m.	♋	♋	♋	♌	♌	♌	♌	♍	♍	♍	♍	♎	♎	♎	♎	♏	♏	♏

Signs	Libra			Scorpio			Sagittarius			Capricorn			Aquarius			Pisces		
Decan	23.09 to 02.10	03.10 to 12.10	13.10 to 22.10	23.10 to 01.11	02.11 to 11.11	12.11 to 22.11	23.11 to 01.12	02.12 to 11.12	12.12 to 21.12	22.12 to 31.12	01.01 to 10.01	11.01 to 20.01	21.01 to 30.01	31.01 to 09.02	10.02 to 19.02	20.02 to 29.02	01.03 to 10.03	11.03 to 20.03
Hours																		
0.00	♋	♌	♌	♌	♌	♍	♍	♍	♍	♎	♎	♎	♎	♎	♏	♏	♏	♏
1 a.m.	♌	♌	♌	♌	♍	♍	♍	♍	♍	♎	♎	♎	♎	♏	♏	♏	♏	♐
2 a.m.	♌	♌	♍	♍	♍	♍	♎	♎	♎	♎	♎	♏	♏	♏	♏	♐	♐	♐
3 a.m.	♌	♍	♍	♍	♍	♎	♎	♎	♎	♏	♏	♏	♏	♐	♐	♐	♐	♑
4 a.m.	♍	♍	♍	♎	♎	♎	♎	♎	♏	♏	♏	♏	♐	♐	♐	♐	♑	♑
5 a.m.	♍	♍	♎	♎	♎	♎	♏	♏	♏	♏	♐	♐	♐	♐	♑	♑	♑	♒
6 a.m.	♎	♎	♎	♎	♏	♏	♏	♏	♏	♐	♐	♐	♐	♑	♑	♑	♒	♓
7 a.m.	♎	♎	♎	♏	♏	♏	♏	♐	♐	♐	♐	♑	♑	♑	♑	♒	♓	♈
8 a.m.	♎	♏	♏	♏	♏	♏	♐	♐	♐	♐	♑	♑	♒	♒	♓	♓	♈	♉
9 a.m.	♏	♏	♏	♏	♐	♐	♐	♐	♑	♑	♑	♒	♒	♓	♈	♈	♉	♊
10 a.m.	♏	♏	♏	♐	♐	♐	♑	♑	♑	♒	♒	♓	♓	♈	♉	♉	♊	♊
11 a.m.	♏	♐	♐	♐	♐	♑	♑	♑	♒	♒	♓	♈	♈	♈	♊	♊	♊	♋

Signs	Aries			Taurus			Gemini			Cancer			Leo			Virgo		
Decan	21.03 to 30.03	31.03 to 09.04	10.04 to 20.04	21.04 to 30.04	01.05 to 10.05	11.05 to 20.05	21.05 to 30.05	31.05 to 09.06	10.06 to 21.06	22.06 to 01.07	02.07 to 11.07	12.07 to 22.07	23.07 to 01.08	02.08 to 11.08	12.08 to 23.08	24.08 to 01.09	02.09 to 12.09	13.09 to 22.09
Hours																		
12.00	♋	♌	♌	♌	♌	♍	♍	♍	♎	♎	♎	♎	♎	♎	♏	♏	♏	♏
1 p.m.	♌	♌	♌	♌	♍	♍	♍	♍	♎	♎	♎	♏	♏	♏	♏	♏	♐	♐
2 p.m.	♌	♌	♍	♍	♍	♍	♍	♎	♎	♎	♏	♏	♏	♏	♏	♐	♐	♐
3 p.m.	♌	♍	♍	♍	♍	♎	♎	♎	♎	♏	♏	♏	♏	♐	♐	♐	♐	♑
4 p.m.	♍	♍	♍	♍	♎	♎	♎	♎	♏	♏	♏	♏	♐	♐	♐	♑	♑	♑
5 p.m.	♍	♍	♎	♎	♎	♎	♏	♏	♏	♏	♐	♐	♐	♐	♑	♑	♑	♒
6 p.m.	♍	♎	♎	♎	♎	♏	♏	♏	♐	♐	♐	♑	♑	♑	♒	♒	♒	♓
7 p.m.	♎	♎	♎	♏	♏	♏	♏	♐	♐	♐	♐	♑	♑	♑	♒	♓	♓	♈
8 p.m.	♎	♏	♏	♏	♏	♏	♐	♐	♐	♐	♑	♑	♒	♒	♓	♈	♈	♉
9 p.m.	♏	♏	♏	♏	♏	♐	♐	♐	♑	♑	♑	♒	♓	♓	♈	♈	♈	♊
10 p.m.	♏	♏	♏	♐	♐	♐	♐	♑	♑	♒	♓	♓	♈	♈	♉	♊	♊	♊
11 p.m.	♏	♐	♐	♐	♐	♑	♑	♑	♒	♓	♈	♈	♈	♉	♊	♊	♊	♋

Signs	Libra			Scorpio			Sagittarius			Capricorn			Aquarius			Pisces		
Decan	23.09 to 02.10	03.10 to 12.10	13.10 to 22.10	23.10 to 01.11	02.11 to 11.11	12.11 to 22.11	23.11 to 01.12	02.12 to 11.12	12.12 to 21.12	22.12 to 31.12	01.01 to 10.01	11.01 to 20.01	21.01 to 30.01	31.01 to 09.02	10.02 to 19.02	20.02 to 29.02	01.03 to 10.03	11.03 to 20.03
Hours																		
12.00	♐	♐	♐	♑	♑	♑	♒	♒	♓	♈	♈	♉	♉	♊	♊	♊	♋	♋
1 p.m.	♐	♐	♑	♑	♑	♒	♓	♓	♈	♉	♉	♊	♊	♊	♋	♋	♋	♋
2 p.m.	♑	♑	♑	♒	♒	♓	♈	♈	♉	♉	♊	♊	♋	♋	♋	♋	♌	♌
3 p.m.	♑	♑	♒	♓	♓	♈	♉	♉	♊	♊	♊	♋	♋	♋	♋	♌	♌	♌
4 p.m.	♒	♒	♓	♈	♈	♉	♊	♊	♊	♋	♋	♋	♋	♑	♌	♌	♌	♌
5 p.m.	♓	♓	♈	♉	♉	♊	♊	♊	♋	♋	♋	♋	♌	♌	♌	♌	♍	♍
6 p.m.	♈	♈	♉	♊	♊	♊	♋	♋	♋	♋	♌	♌	♌	♌	♍	♍	♍	♍
7 p.m.	♉	♉	♊	♊	♊	♋	♋	♋	♋	♌	♌	♌	♌	♍	♍	♍	♍	♎
8 p.m.	♊	♊	♊	♋	♋	♋	♋	♌	♌	♌	♌	♍	♍	♍	♍	♍	♎	♎
9 p.m.	♊	♊	♋	♋	♋	♌	♌	♌	♌	♌	♍	♍	♍	♍	♎	♎	♎	♎
10 p.m.	♋	♋	♋	♋	♌	♌	♌	♌	♍	♍	♍	♍	♍	♎	♎	♎	♎	♎
11 p.m.	♋	♋	♌	♌	♌	♌	♍	♍	♍	♍	♎	♎	♎	♎	♏	♏	♏	♏

STAR SIGNS

Aries

Adventurous, ambitious, impulsive, enthusiastic and energetic. Open to new ideas, loves freedom and welcomes challenges, but can be impatient.

Taurus

A faithful and generous friend, who loves luxuries of every kind. Always follows experiences, but can be stupidly hostile to change.

Gemini

Very intelligent and humane, with a shifting outlook often seeing all points of view. Well-disposed, judicious with a complex, often contradictory, personality.

Cancer

The crab. The hard outer shell conceals a soft and vulnerable interior. Can be badly wounded when they experience disloyalty. Home-loving, with an occult interest.

Leo

A dominant, commanding personality who stands out from the crowd; extrovert and outgoing with great personal magnetism. Very social, but not afraid to bully.

Virgo

Has common sense, practical intelligence and a perfectionist's approach. Loves refinement, cleanliness and order. An outward lack of feeling conceals too much emotion.

Libra

Balance and harmony, sensitive to the needs of others, even tempered. Insatiably curious, with often a chronic inability to make decisions.

Scorpio

An intense personality, with powerful, magnetic attraction. Dignified, reserved in conversation. Easily hurt, quick to detect an insult.

Sagittarius

Has the urge to explore, with a strongly idealistic nature. Needs to feel free; an open and generous attitude to life.

Capricorn

Predictable, stable, serious, independent and strong-willed. Subtle and witty, loves authority, prone to suppress emotions.

Aquarius

Loves liberty and personal freedom; has strong convictions, and seeks the truth. Tend to hide their character and do not make friends easily.

Pisces

Malleable nature, sensitive to feelings, popular, more emotional than rational. Has limited will-power and ambition, and they give more than they take.

BIRTHSIGNS OF FRIENDS AND RELATIVES

Fill in the chart below with your friends' and relatives' birthsigns and you will start noticing character similarities.

ARIES	TAURUS	GEMINI
CANCER	LEO	VIRGO

LIBRA	SCORPIO	SAGITTARIUS
CAPRICORN	AQUARIUS	PISCES

I never wear a medallion with my zodiac sign on it, because many people know at least the basics of the signs, and I wouldn't want anyone I met for the first time to discover a great part of my character just by seeing my sign.

YOUR DAY OF BIRTH

Using the Day of Birth Chart on the next page, look for the column containing your year of birth.

Then, look along the row for your month of birth. At the intersection you will find a number.

Add the date of your birth to this number, and look for the resulting number in the table below: you will find your day of birth.

Sunday	1	8	15	22	29
Monday	2	9	16	23	30
Tuesday	3	10	17	24	31
Wednesday	4	11	18	25	
Thursday	5	12	19	26	
Friday	6	13	20	27	
Saturday	(7)	14	21	28	

Example: you were born on April 6, 1963.

Using the Day of Birth Chart, we find:

Year	January	February	March	April
1963	2	5	5	(1)

1 + 6 = 7: 7 is a Saturday.

You were born on a Saturday.

Day of Birth Chart

Year	Year	Year	Jan	Feb	Mar	Apr	May	Jun
1925	1953	1981	4	0	0	3	5	1
1926	1954	1982	5	1	1	4	6	2
1927	1955	1983	6	2	2	5	0	3
1928	1956	1984	0	3	4	0	2	5
1929	1957	1985	2	5	5	1	3	6
1930	1958	1986	3	6	6	2	4	0
1931	1959	1987	4	0	0	3	5	1
1932	1960	1988	5	1	2	5	0	3
1933	1961	1989	0	3	3	6	1	4
1934	1962	1990	1	4	4	0	2	5
1935	1963	1991	2	5	5	1	3	6
1936	1964	1992	3	6	0	3	5	1
1937	1965	1993	5	1	1	4	6	2
1938	1966	1994	6	2	2	5	0	3
1939	1967	1995	0	3	3	6	1	4
1940	1968	1996	1	4	5	1	3	6
1941	1969	1997	3	6	6	2	4	0
1942	1970	1998	4	0	0	3	5	1
1943	1971	1999	5	1	1	4	6	2
1944	1972	2000	6	2	3	6	1	4
1945	1973	2001	1	4	4	0	2	5
1946	1974	2002	2	5	5	1	3	6
1947	1975	2003	3	6	6	2	4	0
1948	1976	2004	4	0	1	4	6	2
1949	1977	2005	6	2	2	5	0	3
1950	1978	2006	0	3	3	6	1	4
1951	1979	2007	1	4	4	0	2	5
1952	1980	2008	2	5	6	2	4	0

Year	Year	Year	July	Aug	Sept	Oct	Nov	Dec
1925	1953	1981	3	6	2	4	0	2
1926	1954	1982	4	0	3	5	1	3
1927	1955	1983	5	1	4	6	2	4
1928	1956	1984	0	3	6	1	4	6
1929	1957	1985	1	4	0	2	5	0
1930	1958	1986	2	5	1	3	6	1
1931	1959	1987	3	6	2	4	0	2
1932	1960	1988	5	1	4	6	2	4
1933	1961	1989	6	2	5	0	3	5
1934	1962	1990	0	3	6	1	4	6
1935	1963	1991	1	4	0	2	5	0
1936	1964	1992	3	6	2	4	0	2
1937	1965	1993	4	0	3	5	1	3
1938	1966	1994	5	1	4	6	2	4
1939	1967	1995	6	2	5	0	3	5
1940	1968	1996	1	4	0	2	5	0
1941	1969	1997	2	5	1	3	6	1
1942	1970	1998	3	6	2	4	0	2
1943	1971	1999	4	0	3	5	1	3
1944	1972	2000	6	2	5	0	3	5
1945	1973	2001	0	3	6	1	4	6
1946	1974	2002	1	4	0	2	5	0
1947	1975	2003	2	5	1	3	6	1
1948	1976	2004	4	0	3	5	1	3
1949	1977	2005	5	1	4	6	2	4
1950	1978	2006	6	2	5	0	3	5
1951	1979	2007	0	3	6	1	4	6
1952	1980	2008	2	5	1	3	6	1

STAR SIGNS AND THE PLANETS

 Sun: Leo

You are ambitious, enthusiastic, fervent, generous and fair. You are also prone to violence and vindictive behaviour; you look for glory.

Predisposed to: heart pain.

Governs: important decisions, business and professions where authority is needed (magistrates and officers).

Sun people have big personalities, they are majestic, proud, faithful, selfish and stiff. They know how to suffer in silence, are passionate, but often let others down.

 Moon: Cancer

You are passive, receptive, thoughtless, imaginative and a daydreamer.

Predisposed to: intestines, stomach, throat and breast aches.

Governs: home, professions which need imagination or working from home, arts and crafts.

A traveller drawn to strange and mysterious places.
Imaginative, a dreamer with a complex character driven by destiny, likes lonely walks in forests or on beaches.
You are inquisitive, languorous and lazy.
Very devoted, very sweet, rarely satisfied and often disappointed.

Mars: Aries, Scorpio

With a violent nature, you are selfish, irritable, brave, touchy and destructive.

Predisposed to: problems with muscles, gall-bladder, genitals and kidneys, liver aches and blood disorders.

Governs: sports, adventure, struggles and composure.

You are impulsive, energetic and a good leader – often in military or medical careers. However, you have a short temper, like to fight, are jealous and authoritarian.

Mercury: Gemini, Virgo

A mediator, you are adaptable, diplomatic, assimilate easily and have a lot of initiative. You have a melancholic temperament and are stern.

Predisposed to: nervous, spinal chord and foot problems; paralysis, neurosis and hallucinations.

Governs: work, travel, contracts, all professions where skilfulness is needed, such as teaching and creating things.

Quick-tempered, cunning and subtle. Thrifty with a tendency to avarice, you are persuasive, a good liar, cold and love people you can command. If you cheat on your partner, you'll do it cleverly.

Jupiter: Sagittarius, Pisces

This large, good planet bestows felicity and good judgement. You are ambitious, loyal and kind.

Predisposed to: bad liver, blood and circulatory system. You are prone to tiredness.

Governs: money, promotion, law, politics, administration; professions such as priests, policemen and politicians.

Good-tempered, just, honest and careful; you have good self-esteem, you are straightforward, jovial, happy, generous and sensual. If you have an affair, you will always come back to your family.

Venus: Libra, Taurus

Attractive, loving, receptive, sensitive, charitable, kind and indulgent.
Predisposed to: bad backs, bones, pelvis, bladder, leg and foot problems.
Governs: beauty, love, harmony, pleasure and travel.

You are loving, happy and can be frivolous, but also intelligent and quiet. You like to party and to dress well with jewellery and perfumes. Great lovers - passionate but not always faithful, you don't like mediocrity. You expect to be listened to and showered with expensive gifts from your many admirers.

Saturn: Aquarius, Capricorn

Dry, cold and rigid. This planet influences evil, sadness and melancholia.
Predisposed to: fragile bones, spine, articulations, pelvis, bladder, legs, feet and intestinal problems.
Governs: stability, discipline, thriftiness, secret enemies, treachery and false friends.

You are somber, studious, clever and knowledgeable, and often make good doctors and priests. You are also cold, rude, mean and not very good lovers.

PLANETS IN YOUR BODY

Each planet has an effect on your body. The closer to the earth the planet is, the more effect it has on your body and character.

☉	**Sun:**	vitality, heart and spine
☽	**Moon:**	nutrition, digestion and body fluids
☿	**Mercury:**	lungs and nervous system
♀	**Venus:**	throat, kidneys, hormones and ovaries
♂	**Mars:**	red corpuscles, kidneys, hormones and ovaries
♃	**Jupiter:**	growth and the liver
♄	**Saturn:**	the ageing process and bones
♅	**Uranus:**	blood circulation and electricity in the body
♆	**Neptune:**	lethargy
♇	**Pluto:**	transformation, degeneration and sexual organs

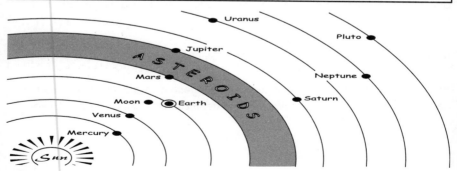

YOUR HEALTH IN YOUR STAR SIGN

Each star sign governs particular parts of the body, and each sign has particular health problems associated with it.

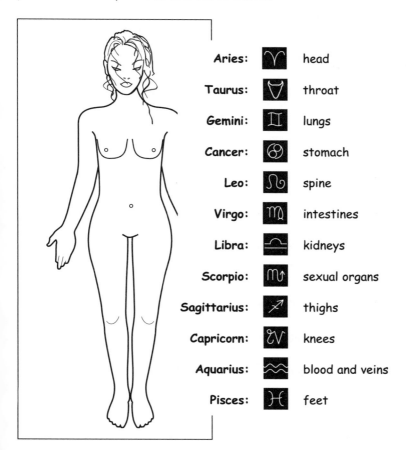

Aries:	♈	head
Taurus:	♉	throat
Gemini:	♊	lungs
Cancer:	♋	stomach
Leo:	♌	spine
Virgo:	♍	intestines
Libra:	♎	kidneys
Scorpio:	♏	sexual organs
Sagittarius:	♐	thighs
Capricorn:	♑	knees
Aquarius:	♒	blood and veins
Pisces:	♓	feet

STAR SIGNS AND PHYSICAL FRAGILITY

Aries	head, brain, headache, nosebleed, congestion
Taurus	throat, laryngitis, thyroid, cholesterol
Gemini	nerves, lungs, shoulders
Cancer	stomach, breast
Leo	heart, high blood pressure, back
Virgo	back, colon, colic
Libra	kidney, bladder, skin, ovaries
Scorpio	sexual organs, infections (sinuses), hormonal problems, period pains
Sagittarius	hips, gall-bladder, liver
Capricorn	articulations, skin, arthritis, sprains
Aquarius	circulatory problems, varicose veins
Pisces	feet, sprains, constipation

ASTROLOGY IN YOUR KITCHEN

Aries: likes to criticize. Always eats too fast. Gulps food down. Will pay the bill. Loves spices.

Taurus: let them choose the wine. Good knowledge of foods. Takes their time to eat. Don't like eating on their own.

Gemini: likes to read or write cookery books. Eats anything, anywhere, very fast, whilst watching television.

Cancer: good cooks. Creators who like to decorate dishes. Like to sit cosily indoors with nice food and wine.

Leo: business lunches in expensive restaurants. The food must be excellent, with the best wines and liqueurs.

Virgo: orderly, clean and neat kitchen. Scheduled meals and times. The table will be nicely set out but without originality.

Libra: subtle, soft atmospheric music and flowers. Lovely decorated tables. Well balanced cocktails and parties.

Scorpio: good critics. Like to decorate with candles and incense. Like mysteries, hot pepper and spices. Do not like to listen to advice.

Sagittarius: loves eating lots of different dishes with lots of friends around. Enjoys cooking. Would love to be the chef or headwaiter on a ship.

Capricorn: doesn't like the responsibility of cooking. Mealtime is always a very serious affair! Loves mother's cooking. Lots of food but not fussy.

Aquarius: nouvelle cuisine. Dreams of owning a fashionable restaurant. Eccentric tastes - likes experimenting and new ideas.

Pisces: intuitive. Knows what's good to eat and where to go and get it! Doesn't mind eating alone, but loves cooking for friends whilst chatting.

Your Astrocake!

	Colour	Taste
Aries:	Red	Strawberries
Taurus:	Green	Kiwi fruit, grapes
Gemini:	Yellow	Pineapple, bananas
Cancer:	Purple	Blackcurrant
Leo:	Orange	Orange, apricot
Virgo:	White	Meringue, vanilla
Libra:	Blue	Blueberries
Scorpio:	Dark red	Dark cherries
Sagittarius:	Mauve	Blackberries
Capricorn:	Violet	Plum
Aquarius:	Dark blue	Black grapes
Pisces:	Pale blue	Blueberries and custard

STAR AFFINITIES

Signs	Friends	Enemies
Aries	Libra, Leo, Sagittarius	Cancer, Scorpio, Pisces, Virgo
Taurus	Scorpio, Virgo, Leo, Capricorn, Aquarius	Cancer, Pisces
Gemini	Libra, Aquarius, Leo, Aries	Pisces, Sagittarius, Cancer, Capricorn
Cancer	Scorpio, Virgo, Pisces	Aries, Taurus, Gemini, Libra, Capricorn
Leo	Libra, Gemini, Sagittarius, Aries	Scorpio, Taurus
Virgo	Taurus, Capricorn, Scorpio, Cancer	Aries, Sagittarius
Libra	Scorpio, Leo, Aries, Gemini, Sagittarius	Capricorn, Cancer, Pisces

Scorpio	Cancer, Taurus, Virgo, Pisces, Libra	Aries, Leo, Aquarius
Sagittarius	Gemini, Aries, Aquarius, Libra	Virgo
Capricorn	Taurus, Scorpio, Virgo	Gemini, Cancer
Aquarius	Gemini, Sagittarius	Libra, Taurus, Scorpio
Pisces	Virgo, Cancer, Scorpio	Libra, Gemini

ASTROLOGICAL SUMMARY

ARIES
Planet: Mars
Character: Anger
Colour: Red
Stone: Ruby
Day: Tuesday
Plants: Lavender, Basil
Metal: Iron
Numbers: 1-4-6

TAURUS
Planet: Venus
Character: Lover
Colour: Green
Stone: Emerald
Day: Friday
Plant: Rose
Metal: Copper
Number: 3

GEMINI
Planet: Mercury
Character: Witch
Colour: Yellow
Stone: Topaz
Day: Wednesday
Plants: Vanilla, Aniseed
Metal: Platinum
Number: 5

CANCER
Planet: Moon
Character: Shy
Colour: Purple
Stone: Pearl
Day: Monday
Plant: Lilac
Metal: Silver
Numbers: 2-5

LEO
Planet: The Sun
Character: Proud
Colour: Orange
Stone: Diamond
Day: Sunday
Plant: Lotus
Metal: Gold
Numbers: 4-7

VIRGO
Planet: Mercury
Character: Seemingly aggressive
Colour: White
Stone: Jasper
Day: Wednesday
Plant: Gardenia
Metal: Platinum
Numbers: 1-5

LIBRA

Planet: Venus
Character: Seducer
Colour: Blue
Stone: Beryl
Day: Friday
Plant: Myosotis
Metal: Copper
Numbers: 1-3-4

SCORPIO

Planet: Mars
Character: Passionate
Colour: Dark red
Stone: Garnet
Day: Tuesday
Plant: Carnation
Metal: Iron
Numbers: 2-6-7

SAGITTARIUS

Planet: Jupiter
Character: Dynamic
Colour: Lavender
Stone: Turquoise
Day: Thursday
Plant: Strawberry
Metal: Pewter
Numbers: 2-4

CAPRICORN

Planet: Saturn
Character: Cold
Colour: Violet
Stone: Onyx
Day: Saturday
Plant: Honeysuckle
Metal: Lead
Number: 1

AQUARIUS

Planet: Saturn
Character: Changeable
Colour: Electric blue
Stone: Sapphire
Day: Saturday
Plant: Iris
Metal: Lead
Number: 1

PISCES

Planet: Jupiter
Character: Intuitive
Colour: Pale blue
Stone: Coral
Day: Thursday
Plant: Jasmine
Metal: Pewter
Number: 4

CHINESE ASTROLOGY

Year	Animal	Start	End
1900	Rat	31-2-1900	18-2-1901
1901	Ox	19-2-1901	7-2-1902
1902	Tiger	8-2-1902	28-1-1903
1903	Cat	29-1-1903	15-2-1904
1904	Dragon	16-2-1904	3-2-1905
1905	Snake	4-2-1905	24-1-1906
1906	Horse	25-1-1906	12-2-1907
1907	Goat	13-2-1907	1-2-1908
1908	Monkey	2-2-1908	21-1-1909
1909	Rooster	22-1-1909	9-2-1910
1910	Dog	10-2-1910	29-1-1911
1911	Pig	30-1-1911	17-2-1912
1912	Rat	18-2-1912	5-2-1913
1913	Ox	6-2-1913	25-1-1914
1914	Tiger	26-1-1914	13-2-1915
1915	Cat	14-2-1915	2-2-1916
1916	Dragon	2-3-1916	22-1-1917
1917	Snake	23-1-1917	10-2-1918
1918	Horse	11-2-1918	31-1-1919
1919	Goat	1-2-1919	19-2-1920
1920	Monkey	20-2-1920	7-2-1921
1921	Rooster	8-2-1921	27-1-1922
1922	Dog	28-1-1922	15-2-1923
1923	Pig	16-2-1923	4-2-1924

1924	Rat	5-2-1924	23-1-1925
1925	Ox	24-1-1925	12-2-1926
1926	Tiger	13-2-1926	2-1-1927
1927	Cat	2-2-1927	22-1-1928
1928	Dragon	23-1-1928	9-2-1929
1929	Snake	10-2-1929	29-1-1930
1930	Horse	30-1-1930	16-2-1931
1931	Goat	17-2-1931	5-2-1932
1932	Monkey	6-2-1932	15-1-1933
1933	Rooster	16-1-1933	13-2-1934
1934	Dog	14-2-1934	3-2-1935
1935	Pig	4-2-1935	23-1-1936
1936	Rat	24-1-1936	10-2-1937
1937	Ox	11-2-1937	30-1-1938
1938	Tiger	31-1-1938	18-2-1939
1939	Cat	19-2-1939	7-2-1940
1940	Dragon	8-2-1940	26-1-1941
1941	Snake	27-1-1941	14-2-1942
1942	Horse	15-2-1942	4-2-1943
1943	Goat	5-2-1943	24-1-1944
1944	Monkey	25-1-1944	12-2-1945
1945	Rooster	13-2-1945	1-2-1946
1946	Dog	2-2-1946	21-1-1947
1947	Pig	22-1-1947	9-2-1948
1948	Rat	10-2-1948	28-1-1949
1949	Ox	29-1-1949	16-2-1950

1950	Tiger	17-2-1950	5-2-1951
1951	Cat	6-2-1951	26-1-1952
1952	Dragon	27-1-1952	13-2-1953
1953	Snake	14-2-1953	2-2-1954
1954	Horse	3-2-1954	23-1-1955
1955	Goat	24-1-1955	11-2-1956
1956	Monkey	12-2-1956	30-1-1957
1957	Rooster	31-1-1957	17-2-1958
1958	Dog	18-2-1958	7-2-1959
1959	Pig	8-2-1959	27-1-1960
1960	Rat	28-1-1960	14-2-1961
1961	Ox	15-2-1961	4-2-1962
1962	Tiger	5-2-1962	14-1-1963
1963	Cat	15-1-1963	12-2-1964
1964	Dragon	13-2-1964	2-1-1965
1965	Snake	2-2-1965	20-1-1966
1966	Horse	21-1-1966	8-2-1967
1967	Goat	9-2-1967	29-1-1968
1968	Monkey	30-1-1968	16-2-1969
1969	Rooster	17-2-1969	5-2-1970
1970	Dog	6-2-1970	26-1-1971
1971	Pig	27-1-1971	14-2-1972
1972	Rat	15-2-1972	2-2-1973
1973	Ox	3-2-1973	22-1-1974
1974	Tiger	23-1-1974	10-2-1975
1975	Cat	11-2-1975	30-1-1976

Year	Animal	Start	End
1976	Dragon	31-1-1976	17-2-1977
1977	Snake	18-2-1977	6-2-1978
1978	Horse	7-2-1978	27-1-1979
1979	Goat	28-1-1979	15-2-1980
1980	Monkey	16-2-1980	4-2-1981
1981	Rooster	5-2-1981	24-1-1982
1982	Dog	25-1-1982	12-2-1983
1983	Pig	13-2-1983	2-1-1984
1984	Rat	2-2-1984	19-2-1985
1985	Ox	20-2-1985	8-2-1986
1986	Tiger	9-2-1986	28-1-1987
1987	Cat	29-1-1987	16-2-1988
1988	Dragon	17-2-1988	5-2-1989
1989	Snake	6-2-1989	26-1-1990
1990	Horse	27-1-1990	14-2-1991
1991	Goat	15-2-1991	3-2-1992
1992	Monkey	4-2-1992	22-1-1993
1993	Rooster	23-1-1993	9-2-1994
1994	Dog	10-2-1994	30-1-1995
1995	Pig	31-1-1995	18-2-1996
1996	Rat	19-2-1996	6-2-1997
1997	Ox	7-2-1997	27-1-1998
1998	Tiger	28-1-1998	15-2-1999
1999	Cat	16-2-1999	4-2-2000
2000	Dragon	5-2-2000	23-1-2001
2001	Snake	24-1-2001	11-2-2002

2002	Horse	12-2-2002	31-1-2003
2003	Goat	1-2-2003	21-2-2004
2004	Monkey	22-2-2004	8-2-2005
2005	Rooster	9-2-2005	28-1-2006
2006	Dog	29-1-2006	17-2-2007
2007	Pig	18-2-2007	6-2-2008

Characteristics of the Signs

RAT:	intellectual skills, charisma, nervousness and a thirst for power
OX:	integrity, stability, eloquence, bigotry, vindictiveness and bias
TIGER:	authority, good luck, bravery, impetuosity and disobedience
CAT:	prudence, longevity, tact, complexity and hypochondria
DRAGON:	success, good health, strength, bravado, mistrust and rigidity
SNAKE:	clairvoyance, intuition, discretion, dissimulation and extravagance
HORSE:	style, popularity, dexterity, selfishness, anxiety and rebellion
GOAT:	sensibility, perseverance, good manners, tardiness and pessimism
MONKEY:	stability, leadership, improvisation, cunning, opportunism and loquacity
ROOSTER:	conservatism, enthusiasm, dissipation, blind faith and bossiness
DOG:	sense of duty, morality, respectability, criticism, cynicism and unsociability
PIG:	honesty, sincerity, culture, credulity, gluttony and hesitation

EGYPTIAN ASTROLOGY

There are twelve signs in Egyptian astrology, each one ruled by a god or goddess.

1	**Amon-Ra**
2	**Anubis**
3	**Bastet**
4	**Geb**
5	**Hapi**
6	**Horus**
7	**Isis**
8	**Nout**
9	**Osiris**
10	**Sekmet**
11	**Seth**
12	**Thot**

JANUARY:	From 1st to 7th	Hapi
	From 8th to 21st	Amon-Ra
	From 22nd to 31st	Nout
FEBRUARY:	From 1st to 11th	Amon-Ra
	From 12th to 29th	Geb
MARCH:	From 1st to 10th	Osiris
	From 11th to 31st	Isis
APRIL:	From 1st to 19th	Thot
	From 20th to 31st	Horus
MAY:	From 1st to 8th	Horus
	From 9th to 27th	Anubis
	From 28th to 31st	Seth
JUNE:	From 1st to 18th	Seth
	From 19th to 28th	Hapi
	From 29th to 30th	Anubis
JULY:	From 1st to 13th	Anubis
	From 14th to 28th	Bastet
	From 29th to 31st	Sekhmet
AUGUST:	From 1st to 11th	Sekhmet
	From 12th to 19th	Horus
	From 20th to 31st	Geb

SEPTEMBER:	From 1st to 7th	Hapi
	From 8th to 22nd	Nout
	From 23rd to 27th	Bastet
	From 28th to 30th	Seth
OCTOBER:	From 1st to 2nd	Seth
	From 3rd to 17th	Bastet
	From 18th to 29th	Isis
	From 30th to 31st	Sekhmet
NOVEMBER:	From 1st to 7th	Sekhmet
	From 8th to 17th	Thot
	From 18th to 26th	Hapi
	From 27th to 30th	Osiris
DECEMBER:	From 1st to 18th	Osiris
	From 19th to 31st	Isis

Characteristics of the Signs

Amon-Ra: You are blessed. The principal Egyptian god governs your destiny. You are the model of power and grandeur. You free yourself from all restraints with disconcerting ease. No one can remain insensitive to your presence and wisdom. You often have a prophetic character but, alas, subtlety is sometimes difficult to comprehend. You never give up. Your altruism makes the happiness of others a priority, and sometimes puzzles those on the receiving end, as you expect nothing in return. In your presence people discover themselves to have hidden talents or vocations. You bring out the best in people. However, to be born under this sign can be both an asset and a handicap. You will need great vigilance and an impeccable moral code. You live life to excess. The light of Amon-Ra shines upon you. Happy are those who cross your path!

Colour: orange (female); yellow (male)

Affinities: Hapi and Horus.

Anubis: Night bird. You are very receptive to the lunar cycle. Attracted to the underworld, you inspire confidence and detest treason. Your lunar tendencies are apt to make you somewhat unstable. You are your own worst critic. Be kinder to yourself and you'll benefit in strength.

Colour: purple (female); sienna (male)

Affinities: Bastet and Isis.

Bastet: Devoted and generous, you possess magnetism and charisma. You can easily become your own guru. You believe that mental power alone can change heaven and earth. You intrigue and fascinate others. The way you speak and view the world gives the impression that you come from somewhere else. You are sensitive to the frailty of others and you are aware that we are merely passing through on this earth. You have too many tendencies to put yourself second.

Colour: grey (female); yellow ochre (male)

Affinities: Sekhmet and Horus.

Geb: Stern and stable. You possess a great sense of organization and practicality. You like things that are concrete and palpable. You inspire confidence and you have the gift of speech and writing. You are the vessel of people's good intentions and good resolutions. Woe to those who do not keep their word. Your anger is terrible. You can be very sensitive, supportive and a good confidant. Your interest in others is a way of side-stepping your own doubts and sufferings.

Colour: reddish orange (female); violet (male)

Affinities: Seth and Horus.

Hapi: You have perfect self-control and a high level of creativity. You appreciate intelligence and beauty. You have great sensibilities and are a dreamer – intuitive and tolerant. You enjoy the sharing of knowledge.

Colours: blue (female); red (male)
Affinities: Amon-Ra and Seth

Horus: You have a clear sense of responsibility and feel that 'he who dares nothing, gains nothing'. Anti-authoritarian, you detest people who succeed by conventional means. You always attack people face on. You are your own worst enemy, but your kindness makes you naïve. Beware, remain modest and you will rule with wisdom.

Colour: gold (female); carmine red (male)
Affinities: Geb and Bastet

Isis: The eternal lover, you stay calm, bring luck and serenity. Be careful less you are too kind and too generous. Your openness and vulnerability for others can lead to your own loneliness. You are suited to astrology, graphology, psychology …

Colours: blue (female); white (male)
Affinities: Osiris and Thot.

Nout: Difficult to get to know, you like to surround yourself with mystery and love to confuse matters. You are very suspicious and fragile. You possess an artistic soul that makes you impressionable and enigmatic. Contemplative, melancholic, you often think 'why me?', but you can also show that you can be incisive and ironic. A lover of life, very fearful and sentimental, love will make you do the impossible. You go straight to the heart of things without bothering with details. You desire perfect equilibrium.

Colours: carmine red (female); brown (male)
Affinities: Amon-Ra and Thot

Osiris: The transmitter of knowledge. You know the answer to every question. You hold the key. You surround yourself with solid people. Know that frivolity will often present itself on your path, but wisdom will always prevail. You are ardent but fragile. You always leave things to the last minute.

Colour: green (female); yellow (male)
Affinities: Isis and Thot

Sekhmet: Pride and vanity. You have a high opinion of yourself. You love and respect religions - for you they represent the source of humanity. However, you are capable of being cold and calculating. You know your limits. You can show yourself merciless. No one can stare you down or win an argument. You are rarely wrong. You like originality and take things seriously.

Colour: turquoise (female); light green (male)
Affinities: Bastet and Geb

Seth: The eternal traveller. You create havoc. You face up to anything, but you don't follow things through. You are more feared than loved, but you know how to forgive and forget. You only remember the good things. Being confident can make you loose touch with reality.

Colour: black (female); turquoise (male)
Affinities: Geb and Hapi

Thot: You enjoy going beyond your own limitations and the whys and wherefores of things. You like to work in peace and quiet. You are self-sacrificing and not afraid to take risks. You are a searcher of truth. Clairvoyant and meditative, your ideas are clear and you have enthusiasm and communicative skills. You despise stinginess and mediocrity. Courageous, you like the fields of medicine and travel.

Colour: white (female); pink (male)

Affinities: Bastet and Isis.

DIVINATION

DIVINATION BY RUNES

ᛚ	Gold	success in life and spirit
ᚢ	Auroch	beginning, strength and power
ᚦ	Giant	managed strength
ᚠ	Cove	inspiration
ᚱ	Car	travel, justice
ᚲ	Seathing	creativity, apparition
ᚷ	Gift	present, magical exchange
ᚹ	Happiness	harmony, joy and cheerfulness
ᚺ	Hail	inner harmony
ᚾ	Need	self-confidence
ᛁ	Ice	self-control
ៃ	Harvest	peace, reward
ᛇ	Yew	initiation
ᛈ	Dice	clarification, change
ᛉ	Protection	protection, caring for others
ᛊ	Sun	hope and success
ᛏ	Star	justice

	Birch	self-sacrifice
ᛒ	Birch	self-sacrifice
ᛗ	Horse	harmony, faithfulness
ᛘ	Man	intelligence
ᛚ	Lake	travel by ship
ᛜ	Peace	inner growth
ᛞ	Day	awakening, ideal hope
ᛟ	Property	prosperity, home
ᛉ	The Verb	universal conscience

This last rune is not used like the others for divination. It is only used as a protection against evil, engraved on a bracelet, or above the front door.

How to read the runes

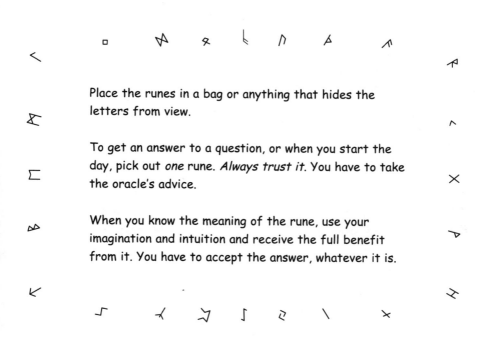

Place the runes in a bag or anything that hides the letters from view.

To get an answer to a question, or when you start the day, pick out *one* rune. *Always trust it.* You have to take the oracle's advice.

When you know the meaning of the rune, use your imagination and intuition and receive the full benefit from it. You have to accept the answer, whatever it is.

Reading for a specific problem

Select 3 runes from the bag.
Put them in front of you and read from right to left:

1. The problem as it is now
2. The difficulties, and what to do about them
3. The result, which you have to meditate on.

Mix the runes up in the bag, without looking at them, and drop them on to the table. Some will be blind. Read the others and follow your intuition to divine their meaning.

Without looking, take as many runes out of the bag as you have letters in your surname. Hold them in your hands. Shake well and drop them on to the table. Some will be blind, some not. Just read and meditate on these you can see.

Other ways of using runes

1. *Pick out 6 runes, three times*
   The first time will analyse the root of the situation.
   The second time will analyse what should happen to you.
   The third time will analyse the present.

2. *Answer by yes or no*
   Throw a handful of runes on a table.
   If the majority is showing: the answer is YES
   If the majority is blind: the answer is NO

3. *Pick up only 6 runes*
   Rune 1:   Will reveal the past, prior to the problem
   Rune 2:   Will reveal the actual problem
   Rune 3:   Will reveal the near future
   Rune 4:   Will reveal the cause of the problem
   Rune 5:   Will reveal the obstacles you will need to overcome
   Rune 6:   Will reveal the final outcome for you to mediate upon

4. *Understanding your destiny (If you believe in reincarnation!)*
   Pick up 5 runes.
   The 1st, 2nd and 3rd speak about your present life.
   The 4th your past life and karmic lesson.
   The 5th outlines your next life in respect of the karma generated in your present life.

Meditate upon the outcome: Life after life, reincarnation of the improved soul (Karma), until perfection is achieved.

COWRIE SHELLS

Cowries are white shells, imported from India to Africa centuries ago. They are thought to hold very strong powers, as well as being used for readings. They were used for decorating clothes, headwear and masks.

If you manage to get your hands on **22 cowries** (sometimes you can find some in African Art shops), make sure they are already cut. You will need to prepare them yourself and they should be used only by you.

Rinse them in clear running water, then in a cup of milk. Dry them, then soak them again in a cup of milk, but this time overnight. Then place them in your lavatory near the toilet bowl (don't ask!)

It will take some time to learn how to read your cowries; for that you will need to get used to handling them every day - touch them, play with them, make them part of you.

There are male and female cowries:

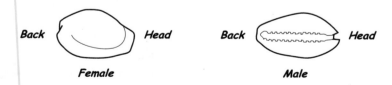

Throw the 22 cowries onto a special carpet or mat on the floor. Cowrie reading can't be done on a table.

If you find 2 female cowries (upside down) very near each other, the reading will be about the past.

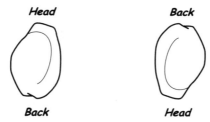

The reading will be about the past

If you find 2 male cowries (upside down) very near each other, the reading will be about the future.

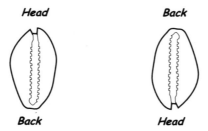

The reading will be about the future

For questions about love, business or health, the answer will always be negative if the cowries look like this:

If two 'heads' are looking at the consultant, he or she will be ill soon. The closer to each other the shells are, the sooner it will be.

Two males, in the same position, heads towards the top, means success.

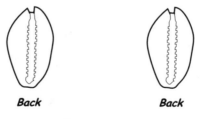

Means success

Two males, in the same position as above, but touching each other, means that the consultant likes to spend all his or her money for nothing!

Two females, in the same position with their heads towards the top, means great happiness.

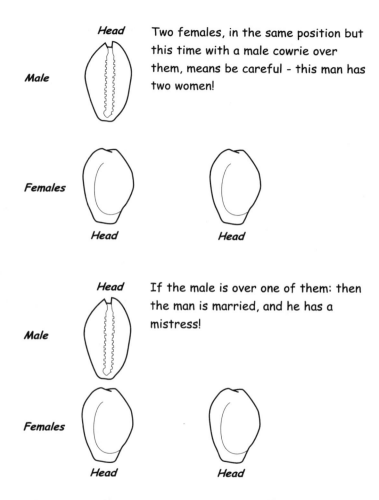

Two females, in the same position but this time with a male cowrie over them, means be careful - this man has two women!

If the male is over one of them: then the man is married, and he has a mistress!

If you are alone and want a quick answer, you can do a reading with 7 cowrie shells only.

READING MATCHES

Throw 10 matches onto the table and, using the chart below read the answer to your question. Use your intuition to translate the answers within the context of your life. With practice, you will understand the matches' message clearly.

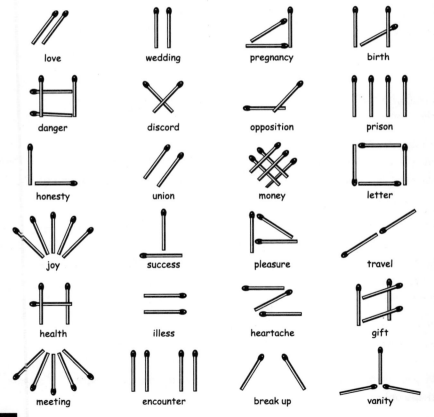

love

wedding

pregnancy

birth

danger

discord

opposition

prison

honesty

union

money

letter

joy

success

pleasure

travel

health

illess

heartache

gift

meeting

encounter

break up

vanity

NUMEROLOGY

1	2	3	4	5	6	7	8	9
A	B	C	D	E	F	G	H	I
J	K	L	M	N	O	P	Q	R
S	T	U	V	W	X	Y	Z	-

Each letter of the alphabet corresponds to a specific number, shown in the chart above.

Spell out your name and surname, and then asign the appropriate number to each letter. The total of the letters is then broken down to give a final number. If, for example, the total of both your name and surname is 26, this should be broken down as 2 + 6 = 8.

The total of the letters, or combinations of certain letters, can reveal a person's character. For example, the total of the complete name reveals the root of the consultant's personality. The total of the vowels in their name, reveal their inner soul; that of the consonants the outer image presented to the world.

Your karmic number is your name and surname:
For example – Kate Smith
This is broken down as: K A T E   S M I T H
                        2 1 2 2   1 4 9 2 8 = 7 + 24 = 31 (3 + 1) = 4
Kate's karmic number is 4.

Your destiny number is your date of birth:

For example - you were born on 25 June 1935

You break it down as: 25 + 6 + 1935

$$(2 + 5 = 7)\ 7 + 6 + (1 + 9 + 3 + 5 = 18)\ (1 + 8 = 9)$$
$$7 + 6 + 9 = 22\ (2 + 2) = 4$$

Your destiny number is 4.

What number are you and what does it mean?

1. You'll always find a solution to problems. Deserved promotion will not be yours unless you claim it. Use tact and diplomacy, go gently as not to hurt people's feelings.

2. Teamwork suits you best, which you would lead of course. You will have to make the extra effort to avoid stagnation. If you fall in love with another 2, don't let your chance go by, as you have so much in common.

3. The number of the trinity. You are a born speaker. You can excel in commercial enterprises where you can be persuasive. Remember that you can also be seduced by the power of your own words, this is your weakness.

4. The number relating to the earth and its solidity. You are the ideal candidate for an enterprise that seeks a model employee, serious and reliable. Positions of trust can be yours and you can expect recognition for your qualities; as you are the only one to doubt them, fight against this shyness.

5. It is the number of motion and evolution. Adventure, research, discovery. You will have the opportunity of earning a living doing what you love best. Don't however throw this opportunity away by giving the impression that you are a flighty person.

6. Whatever your position, you will only be happy if you are the leader. You possess the required qualities - a decisive mind and a sense of equity - to command. Do not forget to be diplomatic as you have the tendency to be abrupt.

7. You watch disputes from afar and whilst everyone is arguing you reap the benefits. This is an advantage which enables you to go far and upwards.

8. This number symbolizes money, success and power. If your partner is also an 8 your ambitions can take you far. Remember that everything that shines isn't gold, and that quality of the heart is worth much more!

9. Without you there would be no doctors, nurses and welfare workers. Don't do more than you can, and do not dictate other people's happiness for them.

Number frequency

Now look for the frequency of numbers - how many 2s, 4s, 5s, etc. occur in you name.

For example, Kate Smith: K A T E   S M I T H

2 1 2 2   1 4 9 2 8

Kate has 1(2), 2(3), 3(none), 4(1), 5(none), 6(none), 7(none), 8(1), 9(1)

Two or more number

1. You have a tendency to count only on yourself. You are over-proud, tyrannical and too self-assured.
2. You tend to count on others for decisions. You are afraid of loneliness and need the approbation of others.
3. You have the tendency to talk too much. Beware of superficial friends.
4. Lack of originality and a rigid way of thinking are signs of an internal blockage preventing you from moving forward.
5. You change your mind all the time. You are always dissatisfied and looking for something else.
6. You are authoritarian. You like to command, consciously or not!
7. You're always thinking about yourself; believing you are the best isolates you.
8. Money, money, money, be careful not to become obsessive.
9. You have the habit of tending to your friend's problems but not your own.

None or only one number

1. You have no confidence at all and you are afraid to start anything. Dig deep to find the courage to correct it.
2. Extreme loneliness. You don't let anyone into your world. You feel isolated especially in love.
3. Extreme shyness. You find it very difficult to talk for yourself and claim what is yours.
4. Daydreamer. Very indecisive. You need inner stability, keep both feet on the ground.
5. You are scared of changes. You like your peace and tranquility. You have an immense need for stability.
6. You run away from responsibility and always have an excuse for your actions.
7. Tendency to not think things through. You opt for futile pursuits and superficial actions.
8. You love spending money. It's a real problem - watch out!
9. You are selfish and indifferent to others. Open your heart.

If you do not have any 2s: this denotes hypersensitivity
If you do not have any 8s: your emotivity is much to high!

PALM READING

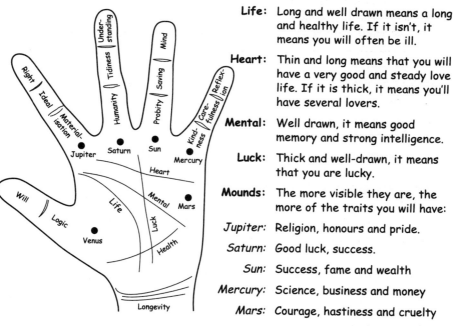

Life: Long and well drawn means a long and healthy life. If it isn't, it means you will often be ill.

Heart: Thin and long means that you will have a very good and steady love life. If it is thick, it means you'll have several lovers.

Mental: Well drawn, it means good memory and strong intelligence.

Luck: Thick and well-drawn, it means that you are lucky.

Mounds: The more visible they are, the more of the traits you will have:

Jupiter: Religion, honours and pride.

Saturn: Good luck, success.

Sun: Success, fame and wealth

Mercury: Science, business and money

Mars: Courage, hastiness and cruelty

Venus: Daydreaming, kindness, love, elegance

The phalanx: The longer they are, the more of their qualities you will have.

If your right hand is itchy - you'll soon be shaking someone's hand

If your left hand is itchy - you'll soon receive money

If your right hand is shaking - someone close to you will be sick

If your left hand is shaking - you'll be invited to a wedding.

USING A PENDULUM

When you first start using a pendulum, you will have to practise every day for at least 15 or 20 minutes to get used to it. Don't expect results straight away!

Ask a very clear question for a yes or no answer. For example: 'Is this tablet good for me?' or 'Should I go on this trip?'

The pendulum will turn clockwise for yes and anti-clockwise for no.

Hold the pendulum over a picture, a map, a certain medicine or anything else you want to know about. Your hand must not move, your wrist must remain very supple and the pendulum will turn by itself.

If, for instance, you misplace something: concentrate, visualize the object, and walk around every room asking the pendulum to find it for you. If the area is too wide or too vague, draw a map to pinpoint the exact location to start the search, and hold the pendulum over it.

If you are asking a question for someone else (for example, is this medicine good for him or her?), hold the pendulum over the object and put your hand on the shoulder of the person you are asking for.

If you haven't got a pendulum, you can use a ring attached to a strand of hair or a piece of thread!

OUIJA

You can draw a Ouija board on a piece of wood and personalize it to your own taste. Never allow children to use or play with it! Do not lend it. It is yours and yours *alone*.

Use a pendulum and breathe deeply - you must be relaxed in a dimly lit and silent room.

Hold your pendulum about 2 or 3 cms above the board and your spirit guide will spell out his or her name to you. Do not be afraid, you'll get use to it! Alternatively, you can use any small object you feel comfortable with, like a glass or one of your favourite stones.

Ask your question. The pendulum will rotate clockwise for 'yes' and anti-clockwise for 'no'. To reveal a date, use the numbers on the board.

If you are a beginner, do not use the Ouija for more than 20 minutes at a time and *never* use it when you are alone!

Always say good bye to your spirit guide by holding the pendulum or stone above 'good bye' and rotating it clockwise.

TAROT

Tarot packs have been used for centuries to foretell the future. The 22 major cards and the four suits are as follows:

GOOD FORTUNE CARDS   **BAD FORTUNE CARDS**

♦
0 The Fool
lack of security
irresponsibility
madness

♦
1 The Magician
creation, will
destiny
initiative

♣
2 The High Priestess
triumph
intuition
understanding

♣
3 The Empress
action
good influence
good wishes

♣
4 The Emperor
awards
generosity
assistance

♣
5 The Hierophant
very important person
protection
good advice

♥
6 The Lovers
choice
romance
indecision

♥
7 The Chariot
triumph
success
promotion

♥
8 Justice
justice,
favourable
answer

♥
9 The Hermit
loneliness
carefulness
dissimulation

♠
10 The Wheel of Fortune
happy change
end of problems

♠
11 Strength
overcome obstacles,
strength of will

♠
12 Hanged Man
bad luck
sacrifices
submission

♠
13 Death
death
end
change

♦
14 Temperance
patience
reflection

♦
15 The Devil
black magic
violence

♦
16 The Tower
accident
depression

♦
17 The Star
occult protection
presentiment

♣ 18 The Moon danger scandal	♣ 19 The Sun success triumph	♣ 20 Judgement birth stability	♣ 21 The World perfection success [the best card]
♥ ace of wands good start creation decision	♥ ace of cups home happiness family	♥ ace of swords triumph pregnancy success	♥ ace of coins work contract intelligence
♠ king of wands protector sincere friendship	♠ queen of wands dark haired helper	♠ knight of wands unexpected departure	♠ page of wands messenger foreigner improvement
♦ 10 of wands money travel [a good card]	♦ 9 of wands lateness annoyance delay	♦ 8 of wands dark girl stability	♦ 7 of wands dark boy celebrity
♣ 6 of wands disappointment bad luck	♣ 5 of wands wealth gold	♣ 4 of wands realization of your plans	♣ 3 of wands start of success

♥ 2 of wands — sadness, loss	♥ king of cups — good friend, devoted man, very important person	♥ queen of cups — kindness, protection, sincerity	♥ knight of cups — new lover, invitation, rivalry
♠ page of cups — young lover, passionate, sincere	♠ 10 of cups — happiness in the family, serenity	♠ 9 of cups — victory, tender, loving but careful	♠ 8 of cups — happy union, rivalry goes away
♦ 7 of cups — seduction, fantasy, friendship	♦ 6 of cups — divorce, separation, nostalgia	♦ 5 of cups — union without love, imperfection	♦ 4 of cups — short deception followed by joy
♣ 3 of cups — happy ending, conclusion	♣ 2 of cups — wedding, good harmony	♣ king of swords — lawyer, intellectual man	♣ queen of swords — evil woman, widow
♥ knight of swords — ambitious young man, troubles	♥ page of swords — spy, enemies, tears	♥ 10 of swords — stab in the back, crises	♥ 9 of swords — death, problems, suffering

♠ 8 of swords difficult situation, illness	♠ 7 of swords cautious hopes	♠ 6 of swords negativity, perilous journey	♠ 5 of swords arguments violence jealousy
♦ 4 of swords doctors hospital abandonment	♦ 3 of swords loss negativity illness	♦ 2 of swords delay movement change	♦ king of coins businessman materialistic
♣ queen of coins practical lady clever	♣ knight of coins sensible man travel	♣ page of coins improvement in finances, ambition	♣ 10 of coins happiness security pleasures
♥ 9 of coins money, success on the way	♥ 8 of coins new job, little money coming in	♥ 7 of coins negativity small journeys	♥ 6 of coins precarious situation
♠ 5 of coins short-term love affair, be careful	♠ 4 of coins gifts trust charities	♠ 3 of coins success chance respect	♠ 2 of coins delay help on way

Tarot reading

The six of any suit is *always* bad fortune:
- 6 of wands signifies the abandonment of plans
- 6 of cups signifies divorce or trickery
- 6 of swords signifies difficult travel
- 6 of coins signifies a perilous situation.

Clusters of three or four cards of the same sort can either be good or bad fortune:

4 aces	luck, good fortune
3 aces	be careful – someone wants to cheat on you
4 kings	you will have the support of men of influence and honour
3 kings	your merit will be talked about
4 queens	you will get together with your loyal and devoted friends
3 queens	there will be chatter, gossip and criticism
4 knights	you will go on a business trip
3 knights	there will be a family outing or gathering
4 pages	fights could be dangerous
3 pages	family talks
4 10s	good and happy changes
3 10s	unforeseen wories
4 9s	happy posibilites
3 9s	success
4 8s	uncertainty, hesitation
3 8s	family happiness
4 7s	enemies
3 7s	birth

Simple readings

Using 15 cards taken from the whole pack, spread them out on a table. Start reading from the top downwards.

For a quick answer to a specific problem, choose 5 cards from the pack at random. Lay them out in a cross.

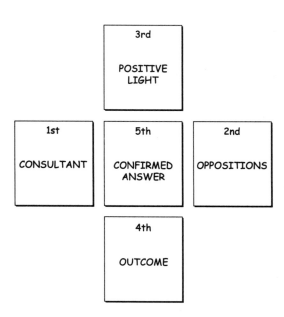

Another method of reading the tarot is to take out 6 cards at random. Reading from left to right, the first two cards concern the past; the next two the present situation; and the final two cards indicate the future.

DOMINOES

Dominoes can be easily used in divination. Pick out at random as many dominoes as letters in your name, turn them over one by one, then read from left to right.

Success in everything	Success if you work hard	This new love is the right one	Luck in money
Luck in your job	Parties, invitations	Illness	
Luck in own business	Bad luck	Good time to redecorate	Divorce or money troubles
Good relationship	Watch your back		
Big success	A baby on the way	Changes in your life	Good business deal
Troubles			
Luck in games of chance	New relationship	Keep your eys open	Arguments
Success in private life	Loneliness	Widow/Widower	
Luck	Short lived happiness		
Nothing new in your life			

If you are reading for someone else, you can put a picture of them on the table and choose three dominoes. Again read from left to right.

You can devise your own methods with practice. The combinations are endless.

GUARDIAN ANGELS

Everyone has a guardian angel, depending upon when you were born. Your guardian angel will protect you, your family, your friends and your home.

Aries	1	March 21-25	Vehia
	2	March 26-30	Jeliel
	3	March 31-April 4	Sitael
	4	April 5-9	Elemiah
	5	April 9-14	Mahasia
	6	April 15-20	Lelahael
Taurus	1	April 21-25	Achaiah
	2	April 26-30	Cahetel
	3	May 1-5	Haziel
	4	May 6-10	Aladiah
	5	May 11-15	Lauviah
	6	May 16-20	Hahaiah
Gemini	1	May 21-25	Iezaiel
	2	May 26-31	Mebahel
	3	June 1-5	Haziel
	4	June 6-10	Hekamiah
	5	June 11-15	Lauviah
	6	June 16-21	Caliel
Cancer	1	June 22-26	Leuviah
	2	June 27-July 1	Pahaliah
	3	July 2-6	Nechael
	4	July 7-11	Yeiayel

	5	July 12-16	Melahel
	6	July 17-22	Aheviah
Leo	1	July 23-27	Nithaiah
	2	July 28-August 1	Haaiah
	3	August 2-6	Jeratel
	4	August 7-12	Seheiah
	5	August 13-17	Reiyel
	6	August 18-22	Omael
Virgo	1	August 23-28	Lecabel
	2	August 29-September 2	Vasariah
	3	September 3-7	Yehviah
	4	September 8-12	Lehahiah
	5	September 13-17	Chavaquiah
	6	September 18-23	Menadel
Libra	1	September 24-28	Aniel
	2	September 29-October 3	Haamiah
	3	October 4-8	Rehael
	4	October 9-13	Deiazel
	5	October 14-18	Hahael
	6	October 19-23	Mikael
Scorpio	1	October 24-28	Veuliah
	2	October 29-November 2	Yelaiah
	3	November 3-7	Sehaliah
	4	November 8-12	Ariel
	5	November 13-17	Asaliah
	6	November 18-22	Mihael

Sagittarius	1	November 23-27	Vehuel
	2	November 28-December 2	Daniel
	3	December 3-7	Hahasiah
	4	December 8-12	Imamiah
	5	December 13-16	Nanael
	6	December 17-21	Nithael
Capricorn	1	December 22-26	Mebahial
	2	December 27-31	Poyel
	3	January 1-5	Nehahiah
	4	January 8-10	Yeialel
	5	January 11-15	Harmel
	6	January 16-20	Mitzrael
Aquarius	1	January 21-25	Umabel
	2	January 26-30	Iah-Hel
	3	January 31-February 4	Anavel
	4	February 5-9	Mehiel
	5	February 10-14	Damabiah
	6	February 15-19	Manael
Pisces	1	February 20-24	Eyael
	2	February 25-28/29	Habuhiam
	3	March 1-5	Rochel
	4	March 6-10	Jabamiah
	5	March 11-15	Haiaiel
	6	March 16-20	Mumiah

ANGELS TO PRAY TO FOR HELP

Before starting, light 3 incense sticks and a white candle:

To be able to pay back money you owe: pray to **St. Albin.**

If you are facing adversity: pray to **St. Baudoin.**

To sell your house at good price: pray to **St. Chronidas.**

Problems with the tax man? Pray to **St. Eusene.**

To be able to stop spending money unnecessarily: pray to **St. Frunence.**

Looking for a job? Pray to **St. Gregoire** or **St. Remi.**

Before an awkward appointment with your boss: pray to **St. Anastase.**

Before an important meeting with your boss: pray to **St. Benoit.**

To stop being too shy: pray to **St. Barlaam.**

If you need more courage: pray to **St. Monas.**

If you want to get married: pray to **St. Estelle.**

For a reconciliation: pray to **St. Bond.**

To stop being jealous: pray to **St. Françoise d'Ambroise.**

To calm a fickle husband: pray to **St. Ella.**

GOOD GENIES

Good genies help you to find or get whatever you want. Like guardian angels, everyone has a good genie, depending upon when they were born.

Aries	1	March 21-30	*Assican*
	2	March 31-April 9	*Senacher*
	3	April 10-20	*Acentacer*
Taurus	1	April 21-30	*Asicath*
	2	May 1-10	*Viraoso*
	3	May 11-20	*Aharaph*
Gemini	1	May 21-31	*Thesogar*
	2	June 1-10	*Versua*
	3	June 11-21	*Tepisatosoa*
Cancer	1	June 22-31	*Sothis*
	2	July 1-10	*Syth*
	3	July 11-22	*Thuimis*
Leo	1	July 23-August 2	*Aphruimis*
	2	August 3-11	*Sithacer*
	3	August 12-22	*Phuonisie*
Virgo	1	August 23-September 2	*Thumis*
	2	September 13-22	*Thopitus*
	3	September 3-12	*Aphut*

Libra	1	September 23-October 2	*Serucuth*
	2	October 3-12	*Aterechinis*
	3	October 13-22	*Arpien*
Scorpio	1	October 23-November 2	*Sentacer*
	2	November 3-12	*Tepiseuth*
	3	November 13-22	*Senciner*
Sagittarius	1	November 23-December 1	*Eregbuo*
	2	December 2-11	*Sagen*
	3	December 12-21	*Chenen*
Capricorn	1	December 22-31	*Themes*
	2	January 1-10	*Epima*
	3	January 11-20	*Homoth*
Aquarius	1	January 21-29	*Oroasoer*
	2	January 30-February 8	*Astiro*
	3	February 9-18	*Tepisatras*
Pisces	1	February 19-28/29	*Archatapias*
	2	March 1-10	*Tnopibui*
	3	March 11-20	*Atembui*

CHARMS FOR LUCK AND PROTECTION

 Padlock for health and happiness

 Key for the realization of projects and longevity of love

 Bell to ward off dangers and for the regaining of health

 Fang for protection against accidents, and gives strength and fertility

 Disc brings luck and is good for games

 Elephant brings success in business

 Fan for health and happiness

 Eye for clairvoyance and lucidity

 Fish for the realization of dreams

 Wheel to regain luck

 Snake for wisdom and longevity

 Tortoise protection against evil

 Clover to bring success and luck

 Magnet to attract luck and good health

 Shoe to protect against enemies

Scissors to cut every malefic influence

Salt contained in a silver pendant, it will protect against black magic

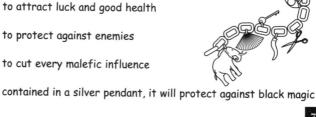

NATURAL MAGIC

CHAKRAS

There are seven chakras within the body. They each govern energy and health, and have different qualities and colours associated with each one.

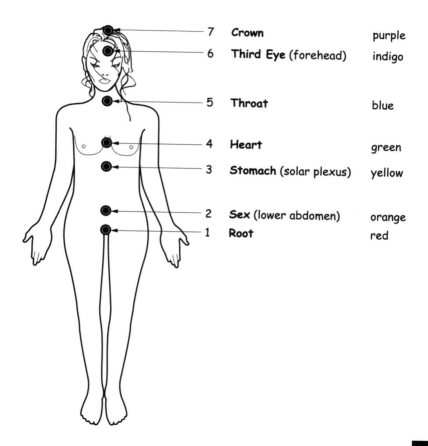

#	Chakra	Colour
7	**Crown**	purple
6	**Third Eye** (forehead)	indigo
5	**Throat**	blue
4	**Heart**	green
3	**Stomach** (solar plexus)	yellow
2	**Sex** (lower abdomen)	orange
1	**Root**	red

Gems and minerals on chakra points

To stimulate the chakras, put the right stone on each point for about 10 or 15 minutes each day.

Before using a stone, put it in clear water for two hours or more. Dry it properly and place it in the sun for further two hours.

Do not allow anyone else to touch your gems.

Always choose a stone that has not been pierced.

When I have a very sore throat and can't swallow, I put a lapis lazuli on the 5th chakra (the Throat) at bedtime and I feel much better the following morning.

Chakra	Colour	Point	Quality	Gem
7	Purple	Crown	Spirituality	Crystal
6	Indigo	Third eye	Intuition	Amethyst
5	Blue	Throat	Inspiration	Azurite
4	Green	Heart	Harmony	Malachite
3	Yellow	Stomach	Intelligence	Agate
2	Orange	Sex	Energy	Citrine
1	Red	Root	Life	Garnet

Essential oils and chakras

The following essential oils are associated with the different chakras:

7 - Crown		*Frankincense, lotus oil*
6 - Third Eye		*Jasmine, vetiver, basil, patchouli, rosemary*
5 - Throat		*Lavender, sandalwood, neroli, sage*
4 - Heart		*Geranium, bergamot, rose, clary-sage*
3 - Stomach		*Camomile, lemon, thyme, ylang-ylang*
2 - Sex		*Sandalwood, petitgrain, ylang-ylang*
1 - Root		*Cedar, clove, cypress, marjoram, myrrh*

Massage direction for the chakra points

Chakras	Male	Female	Effect
7 – Crown	clockwise	anti-clockwise	*for trust in the higher self*
6 – Third Eye	anti-clockwise	clockwise	*brings mental inspiration and understanding*
5 – Throat	clockwise	anti-clockwise	*brings harmony*
4 – Heart	anti-clockwise	clockwise	*for emotional understanding*
3 – Stomach	clockwise	anti-clockwise	*brings peace*
2 – Sex	anti-clockwise	clockwise	*stimulates*
1 – Root	clockwise	anti-clockwise	*calms tension*

YIN OR YANG?

IF YOU ARE YIN
All the massages with essential oils must be done upwards with slow pressure and slow release.

IF YOU ARE YANG
All the massages must be done downwards with quick pressure and quick release.

Are you **YIN**?   or   Are you **YANG**?

Do you hate sports?   Do you like sports?

Do you like chocolate?   Are you an anxious person?

Do you have problems getting up in the morning?   Do you jump out of bed in the morning?

Do you feel tired even after a good night's sleep?   Do you love food?

Do you suffer from stomach aches?   Do you love sweets?

Do you often have backaches?   Do you feel that you are always right?

Are you often stressed out?	Are you a good-humoured kind of person?
Do you walk slowly?	Do you walk very fast?
Are you afraid of falling in love?	Are you always in love?
Do you feel the cold easily?	Do you always feel hot?
Six or more positive answers means that you are **YIN**	Six or more positive answers means that you are **YANG**

ESSENTIAL OILS

Put three to five drops of essential oil in water in a burner if you wish for the following:

Good harmony in your family	**Basil**
To attract money into your business	**Bergamot**
To attract good influences	**Geranium**
Luck and love	**Jasmine**
Peace and serenity	**Lavender**
Protection against enemies	**Lemon**
Calm and harmony in the home	**Orange**
Love and protection	**Myrrh**
Friendship and love	**Rose**
Clairvoyance	**Sandalwood**

If you need help to sleep: *burn three drops of basil.*

Before making love: *put one drop of Ylang-ylang under the tongue.*

To increase the power of meditation and creativity: *place one drop of camomile under the tongue.*

To create a love bath, put two drops of clove essential oil, two drops of ginger, three drops of jasmine and two drops of rose oil into your bath water.

For a money bath, try two drops of cinnamon, two drops of basil and two drops of patchouli essential oils instead.

Essences and herbs in your sign

Star sign	Astral essence	Plants and Herbs
Aries	Lavender	Absinthe, Basil, Pepper
Taurus	Rose	Ginger, Rose
Gemini	Marjoram	Vanilla, Mint
Cancer	Lilac	Sandalwood, Lime
Leo	Vetiver	Angelica, Balm
Virgo	Hyacinth	Gardenia, Acacia, Rose
Libra	Verbena	Musk, Hyacinth, Gladiolus
Scorpio	Heather	Citron wood
Sagittarius	Violet	Amaranth, Strawberry
Capricorn	Honeysuckle	Mint, Narcissus
Aquarius	Fern	Lily of the Valley
Pisces	Wisteria	Jasmine, Peony

PLANETS AND SCENTS

Planet	Day	Sign	Boys' scent	Girls' scent
Moon	Monday	Cancer	Lime	Sandalwood
Mars	Tuesday	Scorpio, Aries	Absinthe	Pepper
Mercury	Wednesday	Gemini, Virgo	Resin	Carnation
Jupiter	Thursday	Sagittarius, Pisces	Peony	Thyme
Venus	Friday	Taurus, Libra	Balm	Musk
Saturn	Saturday	Capricorn, Aquarius	Juniper	Poppy
Sun	Sunday	Leo	Amber	Jasmine

MAGIC PLANTS AND HERBS

Almonds: Always keep a few almonds in your pocket – they attract money, and on days when money is really scarce, burn a few almond leaves along with some incense and, though you'll have to work for it, you will finish the day with money in your hand.

Aneth: Drink as a tea, or you can put a few leaves into your bag: you will feel more attractive and ready to meet someone new.

Aniseed: If you burn it with incense you will feel more positive. If you put some in a blue pouch near your front door, it will bring positive vibes into your home for anyone living in it or visiting you.

Apple: Keep a dry apple in your home and you will always have peace.

Avocado: Growing an avocado in your home will bring luck and creativity.

Basil: If you grow some basil in a pot on your kitchen windowsill it will protect you from evil and negative thoughts.

Cabbage: If you feel depressed for no apparent reason, burn a dry cabbage leaf with some incense and a pale blue candle and you will feel cheered.

Camphor: If you argue a lot in your household, burn some camphor with some incense. However, make sure you leave the room and close the door behind you, as the fumes are quite dangerous and camphor should only be used with caution.

Cloves: If you want to be reconciled with someone, burn some cloves with some incense and your anger will vanish.

Cinnamon: To encourage new friends and happiness in your home, burn some cinnamon, together with three green and four pink candles.

Coriander: If you want something really badly, burn some coriander twice a week and you will get what it is you want. (Be careful of what you want though, as you will get whatever it is!)

Cucumber: If you are really broke, and feel a lot of negativity around you, cut a cucumber lengthways, peel it, and leave it to dry on a plate.

Eucalyptus: If someone is very ill in your household, burn some of this with a picture of the person concerned and an orange candle.

Lemon: If you have drunk too much and feel ill, massage your feet with half a lemon. Do not dry them, but leave it overnight, and you will feel better.

Parsley: This is a very strong aphrodisiac – you should eat some everyday.

Rosemary: Sprinkle a few drops of rosemary oil onto your bed linen to have a peaceful sleep and nice dreams.

Rose: If someone you loved dearly has just died, keep a pink rose by their picture and then burn a stick of incense along with a few of the petals lying around. Your prayers will be heard.

Thyme: Burn one or two leaves with a piece of Mane incense and money will come into your home very soon.

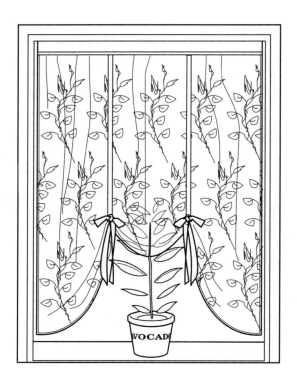

A few years ago my 5-year-old grandson came to see me in the West Indies. One day while we were enjoying a day at the beach, we heard him yelling in the water. A jellyfish had stung him. He had a nasty burn on his leg and was in a lot of pain.

A young girl that lived nearby had heard his screams and knew at once what had happened to him. She disappeared for a few minutes and came back with an Aloe Vera leaf. She broke off a piece of the leaf and applied it to my grandson's leg. In less than two minutes he had stopped crying and was back in the water in no time, enjoying the rest of the afternoon.

The Aloe Vera plant is quite miraculous and is used around the world. It is applied on the skin for burns, cuts and even acne, or drunk for stomach complaints, constipation, period pains and a lot more.

I suggest that, like me, you grow your own plant in your kitchen near a window, and treat it as an emergency first-aid kit!

HONEY

Stomach ache?
Pain in your intestines?   *Try taking buckwheat honey*
Depressed?

Suffering from colds, 'flu, or   *Try thyme or serpolet honey*
Bronchitis?

Tired?   *Try rosemary honey*
Liver complaints?

Insomnia?
Nervous problems?   *Try lime honey*
Rapid heartbeat?

*Replace sugar in teas, cakes and drinks with honey,
and feel the difference!*

INCENSE

Burning incense sticks can attract good things into your life and home. Remember that they should only be burnt in odd numbers at a time (i.e., in ones or threes or fives, etc.). Different scents attract different things:

Amber	Brings protection, luck and money
Cinnamon	For happiness in your home
Citronella	Is strong against enemies
Coriander	For love
Frankincense	Brings success and purification
Hyacinth	For love and luck
Jasmine	It is lucky to burn this as often as possible
Lavender	Promotes harmony and attracts money
Mint	Wards off evil
Mimosa	Gives premonitory dreams
Orange	Helps harmony
Apple	For happiness and success
Rose	Very good to attract love
Sandalwood	Brings luck and good spirits
Vanilla	For luck again
Violet	Brings love, passion and peace.

CANDLES

White	Symbolizes truth, power and realization
Light blue	Symbolizes serenity, happiness, spirituality and protection
Dark blue	Symbolizes depression
Brown	Symbolizes decision-making
Vermilion red	Symbolizes love, attraction and friendship
Dark red	Symbolizes power of mind and existing thought
Gold	Symbolizes attraction, magnetism and persuasion
Yellow-green	Symbolizes jealousy, illness, and anger
Black	Symbolizes sadness, when you have been hurt
Orange	Symbolizes nerves, stimulation, peace of mind, courage and activity
Purple	Symbolizes ambition, victory and great power
Pink	Symbolizes success and honour
Red	Symbolizes love, attraction and vigour
Green	Symbolizes money and wealth

Burn a **red candle** if you are tired and in need of courage, vigour and strength.

Burn a **yellow** one for mental activity, intellect and persuasion.

Purple candles promote calm, serenity and power.

Burn a **light blue candle** if someone owes you money, with some honeysuckle encens as well.

White candles are for purification and benedictions for prayer.

Bright red candles are for sexual attraction, especially if a few drops of coriander essential oil are added.

Green candles attract money into the house.

Burn a **yellow candle** if you need to find a job, or if you need confidence.

Grey candles should be burnt against evil.

Burn **brown candles** if someone is missing.

Gold or **dark blue candles** are good to burn if you need a solution to a problem.

Burn an **orange candle** if you are taking exams.

Burn **purple candles** for power

Pink candles will bring love, affection and calm to the house.

If someone owes you money
burn a light blue candle on a Thursday

For peace and good vibes in your house
burn a pink candle on a Friday

To rid your home of evil
burn a purple candle on a Saturday

To get an answer to a problem
burn a blue candle on a Sunday

To attract money into your home
burn a green candle on a Thursday

To repel evil and black magic
burn a black candle at midnight

To pray with a candle

When you pray, on Mondays light a **light blue candle**.

On Tuesdays light a **red candle**.

On Wednesdays, burn an *orange* one.

On Thursdays try using a **bright blue candle**.

On Fridays, burn a **pink** *or* **light green** one.

On Saturdays, pray with a **dark green** or **purple candle**.

On Sundays, light a **gold candle**.

THE POWER OF THE MOON

If your hair is coloured and you cut it the day of the full moon, it will grow faster.
If your hair is thin, cut it the day of the full moon to thicken it.

In the countryside, wash your white linens on the day of the full moon. Dry them in the open air and they will become whiter! Be careful as it will have the same effect on your coloured garments - they will be bleached whiter too.

Nurses always complain of being overworked on the day of the full moon. For some reason, hospitals are always full on that day.

If you get pregnant when the moon is in a masculine sign (i.e., Aries, Gemini, Leo, Libra, Sagittarius or Aquarius), you will conceive a boy.

When you are working in your garden, plant everything that grows above the ground (salads, fruit trees, etc.) when the moon is ascending. Everything which grows below the ground (potatoes, carrots and other root vegetable) should be sown when the moon is waning.

When the moon is red, nothing will grow in your garden.

The most effective way to lose weight is to fast on the day of the new moon and then again on the day of the following full moon. Only fluids should be consumed on those days.

THE POWER OF THE SUN

Every 11 years, spots appear on the sun which provoke:

A rise in the numbers of epidemics and colds

A rise in the numbers of people suffering cardiovascular problems

A rise in the numbers of people suffering from depression

A fall in energy levels generally

PRACTICAL MAGIC

STRATEGIES TO ATTRACT MONEY

The Moon: Make sure that you always have money in your pocket at the first full moon of spring, and you will have money all year.

Green candle: Anoint a green candle with cinnamon essential oil and burn it on a Wednesday.

Rice: Put some rice in a cup and point it towards the north corner in your home.

Money bath: Combine cinnamon, basil and patchouli essential oils with some liquid soap and use this when you are having a bath.

Wheat: Put a few grains of wheat in your purse.

Camomile: Wash your hands with a camomile infusion before playing any lottery.

Green: Green is a lucky colour - put something green on before going to play any game of chance.

Sugar: Put some sugar in a small bag made of a green piece of material and keep it in your pocket.

Business: If you wish your business to prosper, burn vetiver root, camphor and nine cloves in your shop or office.

Coins: If you find a coin in the street, spit on it before spending it.

Mimosa: If you wear mimosa perfume and burn mimosa incense you will recover any monies owed to you.

LOTTERIES AND GAMES OF CHANCE

Your lucky days to play lotteries and games of chance depend on your star sign.

Aries	Tuesdays and Thursdays
Taurus	Fridays
Gemini	Wednesdays
Cancer	Mondays
Leo	Sundays and Thursdays
Virgo	Wednesdays and Saturdays
Libra	Fridays and Thursdays
Scorpio	Tuesdays
Sagittarius	Thursdays
Capricorn	Saturdays
Aquarius	Saturdays
Pisces	Thursdays

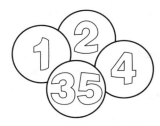

PLANETS, STAR SIGNS AND CAREERS

Each planet governs different characteristics, and the type of career or job you choose will be influenced by these characteristics.

Sun:	The Sun governs individuals' energy and power
Moon:	Governs emotion and imagination
Mars:	Characterizes physical activity and impulsive behaviour
Mercury:	Intelligence
Jupiter:	Honour and money
Venus:	The arts and love
Saturn:	Discipline and pessimism
Uranus:	Inventions
Neptune:	Illusions and spirituality
Pluto:	Self-reflection and destructive behaviour

The types of career suited to each planet and sign are:

Sun (Leo): with the characteristic of authority, careers involving decision-making and jobs requiring business acumen are suitable.

Moon (Cancer): with powers of imagination, arts and crafts and working from home are excellent for you.

Mars (Aries): jobs involving movement, physical activity and self-control are best for those under Mars.

Mercury (Gemini, Virgo): jobs needing quick thinking and accuracy, such as comedians, inventors and teachers, would idealy suit you.

Jupiter (Sagittarius): careers involving money, law, politics and administration.

Venus (Libra, Taurus): working with beautiful things, such as in the arts or show business, would suit you best.

Saturn (Capricorn): jobs which do not involve much change and uncertainty, and which require concentration: working on the land would be ideal.

Uranus (Aquarius): careers which encourage free-thinking, understanding and communication.

Neptune (Pisces): working with people is your forté; try psychology or public relations, or even photography.

Pluto (Scorpio): Pluto, the ruler of the underworld, pushes you towards careers involving taxes and legal (or illegal) matters.

STRANGE BUT TRUE!

When I lived in the West Indies, I had a very nice neighbour. One day I met her in the street and could see that she had been crying. After 18 years of marriage, her husband had left her for someone else, a younger model at that! A month later I met her again, but this time she was smiling and looking really happy. I just had to find out what had transformed her in such a short space of time. She told me the whole story.

She was 'advised' to put her husband's pillow in the middle of their bed, every evening before bedtime, hit it with her fist very hard and repeat loudly: 'Pillow, pillow, pillow, it is not you I am hitting but "X"'s [her partner's name] head, to make him see sense and understand that he has to come back home!' Then she took a chair and dragged it behind her through every room of their house, saying: 'Chair, chair, chair, it is not you I am dragging but "X"'s spirit, to make him come back where he belongs.'

After a week, he came back, apologizing for his behaviour, and bringing jewellery, flowers and a whole new set of furniture for his wife!

I used to suffer from extremely painful cramps. I had tried everything and was at the end of my tether. One day my boss told me that his globetrotting aunt use to carry a bar of soap called 'Savon de Marseilles' in her luggage everywhere she went. I was quite puzzled because it isn't a particularly nice-looking or sweet-smelling soap. I was intrigued and sceptical, but he said that she swore by it. All she did was slip it in her bed at night and put her feet on it! She never suffered from cramps again. That same day I was the proud owner of a bar of 'Savon de Marseilles', and I too enjoyed my first cramp-free night for ages!

If you see a rainbow do not point at it with your finger - it is unlucky.

☆ ☆ ☆

If you light a candle and it starts to smoke, you will receive some news.

☆ ☆ ☆

If you break an egg by mistake it's a sign of happiness, but if the egg is rotten it is a forewarning of someone's death.

☆ ☆ ☆

In India, if a woman sees a shooting star when she is around five months pregnant, she will have a difficult child!

PENTACLES

I have been preparing pentacles to order for 18 years. You cannot get an efficient one over the counter; it has to be made especially for you on a piece of parchment paper (or a medal). It should be written in Hebrew with your star sign, planets and what you requested the pentacle for, i.e., love, money, career or health.

A friend of mine in her 50s had been a widow for a number of years and was desperately lonely. She asked me if I could do anything to help her and so I prepared a pentacle for her. I was her maid of honor the following year!

APHRODISIACS

The following all act as aphrodisiacs:

Rub two drops of sandalwood, Ylang-ylang, rosemary or rose essential oils on your body after your bath.

Drink a small glass of water with three drops of savory, cinnamon, coriander, nutmeg, clove, ginger, mint or wild marjoram in it.

If you are a man, massage your stomach and back with two drops of juniper essential oil.

Burn the following essential oils neat at night on your bedside cabinet: sandalwood, rose, jasmine or geranium.

Drink a (not too hot) cup of herb tea of rosemary, citronella and cinnamon.

Place three drops of patchouli and three drops of Ylang-ylang into a hot bath.

Mix three drops of ginger and three drops of mountain savory in a large glass of cold water and ice, for a long, cool drink.

The following incenses are aphrodisiacs: aphrodisia, coriander, musk, or patchouli.

The colour blue symbolizes attraction – so wear something blue when you go out.

Burn golden-yellow or red candles, which symbolize passion.

The verb: to love

> Its past is not simple
> Its present is only indicative
> Its future is always conditional.
>
> *(Jean Cocteau)*

We can change our attitude toward the past

The past is over and done with.
We can not change that now.
How foolish of us to punish ourselves in the present
because someone hurt us in the distant past.
Begin to dissolve the resentment now.
It is vital that we release these negative ideas.

*TO RELEASE THE PAST, WE MUST BE
WILLING TO FORGIVE*

BABIES

If you want to have a **boy**, try getting pregnant at the time of the new moon, and try eating and drinking those items listed in the left-hand column below; avoid eating the items in the right-hand column:

Eat and Drink	**Avoid**
Tea, coffee and sodas	*Mineral water*
Fruit juices, wine and beer	*Milk, cheese and dairy products*
Meat, smoked and canned fish	*Shellfish, snails and cod roe*
Eggs, once a week	*Cereals, wholemeal flour and pancakes*
Pastas and semolina	*Wholemeal bread*
Bread, white flour and rice	*Green salad*
All kinds of fruits	*Cabbage*
Sugar, honey and jams	*Mustard*
Oil, butter	*Cream*
Biscuits, dark chocolate	*White chocolate*
Olives and jerkins and soups	*Vegetables*

If you want to have a **girl**, try getting pregnant seven days before full moon. Again, here are a list of items you should eat and drink, and some to avoid.

Eat and Drink	**Avoid**
Milk, fruits	Tea, coffee and fruit juices
Spicy food	Crabs
Mineral water	Pizzas, dried fruits
Fresh fish and meat	Pineapple, oranges and melons
Eggs, yoghurts	Sugar, honey and jams
Unsalted bread	Oil and butter
Pastas, rice	Biscuits, cheese, salted bread
Vegetables	Croissants, cakes

IF YOU ARE PREGNANT, AVOID FENNEL!

GRANTING OF WISHES

You should pray for wishes to be granted only when the moon is ascending and the hour is right:

January	13.00-13.45	18.00-18.45
February	13.00-13.50	18.50-19.40
March	13.00-14.00	20.00-21.00
April	13.35-13.40	20.00-21.15
May	13.20-14.40	22.40-24.00
June	12.45-14.10	22.50-00.10
July	13.20-14.40	22.50-00.10
August	12.50-14.00	19.55-21.00
September	12.20-13.20	19.20-20.20
October	12.05-12.55	17.55-18.45
November	12.15-12.55	17.55-18.45
December	12.20-13.00	17.00-17.40

If you are praying for money, pray to Michael on a Sunday only.

If you need luck, pray to Sachiel only on Saturdays.

For health, pray to Samuel on Thursdays only.

If you are looking for love, pray to Anael only on a Friday.

For success, pray to Raphael on Wednesdays.

If you want to travel, pray to Gabriel on Mondays only.

> DON'T EVER PRACTICE **BLACK MAGIC!**
>
> THE BOOMERANG EFFECT IS ALWAYS 10 TIMES WORSE THAN WHAT YOU ORIGINALLY ASKED FOR.

HEALTH

For general good health: Burn lavender and basil in the house. In winter three drops of essential oil of thyme in bowl of hot water on the radiator will ward away colds and coughs. Or you can do what I used to do when I was in France. During the winter my children (brought up in Africa) were not accustomed to the cold. So I would put five or six drops of Eucalyptus essential oil in a bowl or on the radiator in their room for cold and cough prevention.

Toothache: Wear a small red silk bag somewhere on you, containing sea salt and a piece of crumbled charcoal.

Rheumatism: A small ivory ball placed under your pillow will help to ease rheumatism.

Kidneys: A dry cherry stone worn as a pendant around your neck will help if you have problems with your kidneys.

Sleep: To help you sleep, warm your hands, put two drops of essential oil of basil in your palm and massage your body as soon as you go to bed.

Stomach ache: To get rid of stomach ache, soak some coriander seeds and rice in water overnight; cook and eat it the following morning.

Digestion and hard arteries:	Garlic tea aids digestion and helps to prevent hardened arteries.
Sprains:	Massage the sprained joint with three cloves of garlic mixed with oive oil.
Ulcers, eczema, burns and sprains:	Use a compress of cabbage to help relive the pain.
To clear your chest:	Drink a cup of thyme tea every morning.
Insect bites:	Use a compress of parsley on these (parsley also helps you if you are anaemic).
Memory:	To help improve your memory, place an azurite gem on your 6th chakra (Third Eye) for 15 minutes every morning. Or you can put a small sprig of rosemary in toilet water and massage the 7th chakra (the Crown) for one or two minutes each morning.

Gemstones and health

Crystals, precious stones and gems are wonderful for a whole range of conditions:

Agate	Heart, pain and deafness
Amethyst	Calm, sleep, stomach, eyes, headache, eczema
Aventurine	Heart, eczema, skin problems
Chalcedony	Depression, bleeding, apoplexy, poisoning
Cornelian	Cramps, high blood pressure, rheumatism, fever
Crystal	Diarrhoea, backaches, seasickness, bleeding
Falcon eye	Bends, respiratory tracts, asthma
Tiger eye	Asthma, colds, cramps
Heliotrope	Haemorrhoids, intestinal cramps, nosebleeds
Hematite	Cramps, sleep, anaemia
Jasper	Morning sickness, bladder, stomach
Lapis-lazuli	Throat, hair, eczema, apoplexy
Malachite	Heart, arthritis, diuretic, eyes, periods
Smoked quartz	Nervous problems, smokers
Pink quartz	Thymus, emotional problems
Turquoise	Liver

Physical health

Calming	all green stones
Revitalizing	all orange stones
Stimulating	all red and pink stones

Mental health

Calming	all indigo and green stones
Revitalizing	emerald, lapis lazuli
Stimulating	all yellow and purple stones

Spiritual health

Calming	pale blue and blue sapphires
Revitalizing	golden and pink stones
Stimulating	purple and indigo

Give yourself a few minutes every day to sit in quiet meditation. If you are new to this begin with five minutes.

Sit quietly, observe your breathing and allow thoughts to pass gently through your mind. Give them no importance, and they will pass on.

It is the nature of the mind to think, so do not try to get rid of thoughts.

We create every so-called 'illness' in our body.
The body, likes everything else in life, is a mirror of our inner thoughts and beliefs.
The body is always talking to us, if we will only take the time to listen.

Every cell within your body responds to every single thought you think and every word you speak.

PROTECTION

There are many ways that you can protect yourself, your family and your home against dangers and evil:

Your bed: Make sure that you sleep with your head to the north and your feet to the south. Never lie with your feet towards the door, but your head instead (evil spirits cannot count your hair).

Charcoal: Put three pieces of charcoal on a small plate, in a corner of each room and under your bed. After three days burn the pieces without touching them and replace them. After another three days, burn and replace them again. Then, the third time, leave them on the plates (where nobody can see them).

Broomstick: Before going to bed, put a broom upside down by the front door. When you get up in the morning, don't forget to put it back the right way up. If you want someone to leave your home: do the same as before. Then put the broom away as soon as the person has left.

Cloves: Place three cloves by your front door, three by the sitting-room door, and three by your bedroom door.

Fresh Basil:	Evil hates basil, so keep a pot of fresh basil outside your front door, and in your kitchen.
Sandalwood:	Sprinkle around a room three drops of sandalwood essential oil and some sea salt dissolved in water.
Tiger's eye gemstone:	Place the stone above the front door after you have cleaned the stone in water all night and, in the morning, left it for two hours in the sun.
Incense:	Burn lavender or jasmine incense to bring peace in your house.
Protection incenses:	Incenses which should be burnt to bring protection are frankincense, sandalwood, rosemary, myrrh, juniper, clove and cinnamon.
Protection bath:	Dissolve two drops of essential oil of cinnamon, three drops of essential oil of rosemary and two drops of essential oil of lavender in the water.
Pillow:	Sprinkle sea salt mixed with sandalwood on your pillow.
Black cat:	A black cat is very good to have about the house: they absorb any negativity.
New house:	When you move into a new house, always enter first with bread and salt.

More protection

Fern: placed in a pot in your sitting room it turns down negativity.

Garlic: to hang above your kitchen door.

Prickle: keep a prickle from a red rose in your purse or wallet.

Nutmeg: keep a pealed nutmeg in your pocket; hold it, play with it and smell your hand – it protects against arguments.

Sage: sage placed by the front door takes away bad luck.

Nails: hammer nails into a wooden board, or into a cork and put them under your bed, against the wall – they will repel all negative thoughts and vibes directed against you.

Cloves: burn cloves for happiness and understanding in your environment.

Mint: put a few drops of mint essential oil on a sugar cube if you're feeling angry – it will calm you.

Try to avoid giving a picture of yourself to a person whom you instinctively mistrust - you never know what they will do with it!

Inviting friends for dinner? Make sure you don't have 13 guests around the table.

If you do, one of your guests (or even yourself) will be sick, or some kind of ill fortune will happen to them.

Cats

Having a cat is a good protection. Cats are able to see ghosts, and they absorb negativity in your home.

In France, we say that cats have seven lives:

1. *the mistrust of Saturn*
2. *the vitality of Jupiter*
3. *the sensuality of Venus*
4. *the aggressiveness of Mars*
5. *the shrewdness of Mercury*
6. *the independence of the Sun*
7. *the intuition of the Moon*

The other two lives must be for luck!

Moving into a new house

When you move house, before moving anything in place in the middle of each room a glass dish, containing two or three cloves of garlic and two or three pieces of charcoal.

After three days put everything in the bin. Do not touch the garlic or charcoal, but drop the pieces in very carefully; then burn sticks of incense (frankincense, sandalwood, rosemary or juniper).

The following day, start to move a table into the sitting room or kitchen. Never, ever, start moving in furniture with a bed - you, or someone in the house, will often be ill if you do this.

If you happen to feel uncomfortable in a room, put 27 pieces of rock sea salt in a copper dish, add seven teaspoons of any sort of alcohol, and set it alight with a wooden match. If it makes a crackling noise, there was a lot of negativity in the room. The noisier it is the more negativity there was!

INAUSPICIOUS DATES

The following days are very inauspicious for the activities listed, and should be avoided if at all possible.

Weddings:	Tuesdays 6th or 7th
Important purchases:	Fridays or Saturdays 8th
First dates:	Mondays or Tuesdays 2nd or 9th
Important meetings:	Mondays or Saturdays 7th
Hiring people:	Tuesdays 1st, 2nd or 4th
Giving a reception:	Tuesdays 1st or 9th
Cultural activities	Mondays 3rd
Arguments:	Wednesdays 7th

WEDDING ANNIVERSARIES

1st:	Cotton	*14th:*	Ivory
2nd:	Paper	*15th:*	Crystal
3rd:	Leather	*20th:*	China
4th:	Flower	*25th:*	Silver
5th:	Wood	*30th:*	Pearl
6th:	Sugar	*35th:*	Coral
7th:	Wool	*40th:*	Ruby
8th:	Pottery	*45th:*	Sapphire
9th:	Earthenware	*50th:*	Gold
10th:	Tin	*55th:*	Emerald
11th:	Steel	*60th:*	Diamond
12th:	Silk	*70th:*	Platinum
13th:	Lace	*80th:*	Oak

PYRAMIDS

Pyramids are very special shapes, with lots of magical power attached to them.

The first thing to do is to build yourself a pyramid out of cardboard, plastic or anything else you find pliable but durable enough. It should be at least 30cms square at the base and hollow; it will become your everyday tool, and may even protect you!

If you have a car, you can place your pyramid on its bonnet at night, and you will be surprised to find that your engine will be in top working condition for a very long time! You can also stick a tiny pyramid on your dashboard to protect you from accidents!

Hang the pyramid above plants to improve their growth and their leaves will shine. To ripen fruits and vegetables place them under the pyramid for an hour; they will then be ready to eat!

To get rid of the sourness of lemon juice, put the lemons under the pyramid.

To make orange juice sweeter put it under it too.
To remove the bitter taste in your freshly brewed coffee, place the cup underneath.
Place your knives, scissors etc. under your pyramid overnight - they will be sharper in the morning.

If you have a special wish or request, write it on a small piece of paper and put it under the pyramid. Your wish will come true!

I have tried all of these, and it really does work.